KU-566-415

THE WORLD CUP
A COMIC BOOK
HISTORY

Written by
WILLIAM WALKER

Illustrated by
DAVID MOFFAT

Queen Anne Press

First published in 1993 by Queen Anne Press
a division of Lennard Associates Ltd
Mackerye End
Harpenden
Herts AL5 5DR

© William Walker and David Moffat 1993

ISBN 1 85291 530 7

British Library Cataloguing in Publication Data is available

All rights reserved. No part of this publication may be reproduced, stored in a retrieval system, or transmitted, in any form or by any means, without the prior permission in writing of the publisher, nor be otherwise circulated in any form of binding or cover other than that in which it is published and without a similar condition including this condition being imposed on the subsequent purchaser.

Cover design by Cooper Wilson

Printed and bound in Slovenia

ACKNOWLEDGEMENTS

The authors would like to thank all the journalists and authors who have written books and articles on the World Cup. Particular acknowledgement is due to Ian Morrison, Jack Rollin, Brian Glanville, Keir Radnedge, John Robinson and Simon Inglis – all of whom have made splendid contributions to the subject and to football literature in general.

Thanks also to the following:
FIFA, World Cup USA 1994, the Dutch FA, Adrian Stephenson at Lennard/Queen Anne Press for his enthusiasm and patience, John Pawsey and Andy Meikleham for their assistance and a special thanks to Lynne, Lynne and Glenn for their support.

JULES RIMET
President
Fédération Internationale de Football Association
1921-1954

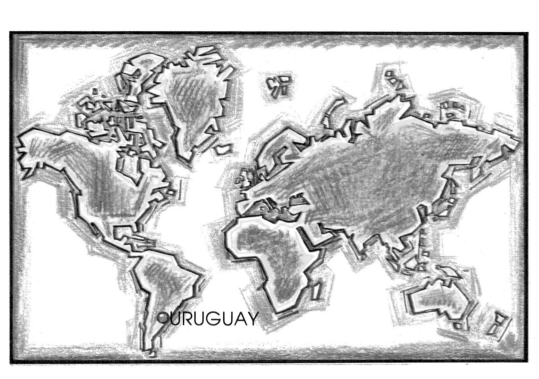

URUGUAY

1930 URUGUAY

BARCELONA, MAY 1929. AT A MEETING OF **FIFA** - WORLD SOCCER'S GOVERNING BODY - THEIR PRESIDENT **JULES RIMET** FINALLY GETS THE SEAL OF APPROVAL FOR HIS LONG-STANDING DREAM - A **GLOBAL** SOCCER TOURNAMENT.

URUGUAY, HOME OF THE REIGNING OLYMPIC CHAMPIONS IS SELECTED FOR THE **FIRST-EVER** 'WORLD CUP'. THE HOSTS BUILD A BRAND NEW STADIUM IN THE CENTRE OF MONTEVIDEO.

THE WINNERS WILL RECEIVE A 32 CM HIGH **SOLID GOLD** CUP. IT LATER BECOMES KNOWN AS THE 'JULES RIMET TROPHY'.

DESPITE URUGUAY'S OFFER TO PAY THEIR EXPENSES, ONLY **FOUR** EUROPEAN COUNTRIES UNDERTAKE THE **THREE-WEEK** STEAMER JOURNEY TO SOUTH AMERICA. ONE OF THESE IS **ROMANIA** WHOSE TEAM IS PICKED BY THEIR FOOTBALL-LOVING MONARCH, KING CAROL.

ON 13 JULY 1930, THE WORLD CUP BEGINS. LUCIEN LAURENT OF **FRANCE** SCORES THE TOURNAMENT'S FIRST-EVER **GOAL** AS HIS TEAM BEAT MEXICO 4-1.

IT'S NOT LONG BEFORE **CONTROVERSY** REARS ITS HEAD. IN FRANCE'S NEXT GAME, AGAINST ARGENTINA, THE REFEREE **BLOWS** FOR FULL TIME SIX MINUTES **EARLY** - JUST AS LANGILLER LOOKS SET TO EQUALISE. THE FRENCH **LOSE** 1-0.

IN THE ARGENTINA-CHILE MATCH, A **FIGHT** BREAKS OUT AFTER A BAD FOUL BY ARGENTINIAN CENTRE-HALF MONTI. **POLICE** HAVE TO SEPARATE THE COMBATANTS.

SURPRISE PACKETS OF THE COMPETITION ARE THE **USA** WHO ADVANCE BY DEFEATING BOTH BELGIUM AND PARAGUAY 3-0. THEY ARE TAGGED **'THE SHOT-PUTTERS'** ON ACCOUNT OF THEIR BULKY BUILD.

'All the world's a stage' - William Shakespeare

ON THE EVE OF THE FINAL, BOATLOADS OF ARGENTINIAN FANS CROSS THE RIVER PLATE AND THERE IS **TENSION** AS THE POLICE SEARCH THEM FOR WEAPONS.

BUT THE AMERICANS' **LIMITATIONS** ARE EXPOSED IN THE SEMI-FINAL AND THEY **CRASH** 6-1 TO THE EXPERIENCED ARGENTINA SIDE. HOSTS URUGUAY WIN THEIR SEMI BY THE SAME SCORE TO SET UP A **CRUNCH** MATCH BETWEEN THE TWO **ARCH-RIVALS.**

THE MATCH BEGINS AND AFTER 12 MINUTES URUGUAY DRAW **FIRST BLOOD.** DORADO SCORES WITH A **POWERFUL** DRIVE.

BEFORE THE KICK-OFF THERE IS **MORE DRAMA** - BOTH SIDES WANT TO USE THEIR **OWN** BALL. THE REFEREE, COMPLETE WITH PLUS-FOURS, ARBITRATES BY TOSSING A COIN.

HOWEVER, THE ARGENTINIANS **FIGHT BACK** STRONGLY. PEUCELLE EQUALISES AND, EIGHT MINUTES BEFORE THE BREAK, STABILE **POACHES** A GOAL TO GIVE THE VISITORS A 2-1 LEAD.

IN THE SECOND HALF, URUGUAY'S TECHNICAL SUPERIORITY SEES THEM **DOMINATE** ONCE MORE. THEY SCORE TWICE TO GO AHEAD AND, IN THE **FINAL MINUTE,** THE ONE-HANDED CASTRO SEALS VICTORY.

THE **HOME TEAM** ARE WORTHY CHAMPIONS - MONTEVIDEO GOES **WILD.**

BUT THE RESULT IS NOT SO WELL-RECEIVED IN BUENOS AIRES. **FURIOUS** ARGENTINIAN FANS **STONE** THE URUGUAYAN EMBASSY.

THE WORLD CUP HAS **WELL AND TRULY** ARRIVED!

'Other countries have their history - Uruguay has its football' - Ondino Viera, Uruguay manager 1966

Pool 1

	P	W	D	L	F	A	Pts
Argentina	3	3	0	0	10	4	6
Chile	3	2	0	1	5	3	4
France	3	1	0	2	4	3	2
Mexico	3	0	0	3	4	13	0

Pool 2

	P	W	D	L	F	A	Pts
Yugoslavia	2	2	0	0	6	1	4
Brazil	2	1	0	1	5	2	2
Bolivia	2	0	0	2	0	8	0

Pool 3

	P	W	D	L	F	A	Pts
Uruguay	2	2	0	0	5	0	4
Romania	2	1	0	1	3	5	2
Peru	2	0	0	2	1	4	0

Pool 4

	P	W	D	L	F	A	Pts
USA	2	2	0	0	6	0	4
Paraguay	2	1	0	1	1	3	2
Belgium	2	0	0	2	0	4	0

Semi-finals

Argentina	6	USA	1
Uruguay	6	Yugoslavia	1

Final

Uruguay	4	Argentina	2

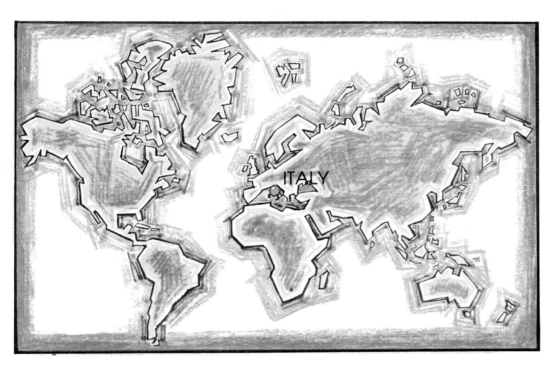

ITALY

1934 ITALY

ITALY IS CHOSEN TO **HOST** THE 1934 TOURNAMENT. THEIR NATIONAL LEADER **MUSSOLINI** SEES THE WORLD CUP AS THE PERFECT OPPORTUNITY TO PROMOTE HIS **FASCIST** REGIME.

CAMPIONATO MONDIALE DI CALCIO

WITH 32 ENTRIES, A **QUALIFYING** COMPETITION HAS TO BE HELD. THIS THROWS TOGETHER THE FIRST-EVER **CONTENDERS** FROM AFRICA AND ASIA - EGYPT AND PALESTINE RESPECTIVELY.

AMAZINGLY, MEXICO **TRAVEL** TO EUROPE AND, AFTER A QUALIFYING ROUND DEFEAT BY THE USA, SAIL FOR HOME WITHOUT PLAYING EVEN A **SINGLE** MATCH IN THE FINALS!

THE TOURNAMENT IS BASED ON A STRAIGHT **KNOCK-OUT** FORMAT. HOSTS ITALY, BOLSTERED BY THREE ARGENTINIAN 'IMPORTS', BEGIN WITH A 7-1 THRASHING OF THE USA.

DOMESTIC PROBLEMS MEAN THE **ABSENCE** OF WORLD CUP HOLDERS URUGUAY WHILE THE 1930 RUNNERS-UP ARGENTINA SEND A VIRTUAL **THIRD-CHOICE** TEAM. THEY ARE AFRAID OF LOSING MORE PLAYERS TO THE **LIRA-LADEN** ITALIAN CLUBS.

ARGENTINA LOSE TO A **WORKMAN-LIKE** SWEDEN AND THE SOUTH AMERICAN CHALLENGE ENDS WHEN BRAZIL **MISS** A PENALTY AND GO DOWN 3-1 TO SPAIN IN GENOA.

IN THE QUARTER-FINALS, FLORENCE STAGES TWO **BRUISING** ENCOUNTERS BETWEEN SPAIN AND ITALY WHO **EVENTUALLY** WIN THROUGH AFTER A REPLAY.

IN MILAN, THE ITALIAN *AZZURRI* (BLUES) THEN COME UP AGAINST AUSTRIA'S *WUNDERTEAM* - MANY PEOPLE'S PRE-TOURNAMENT **FAVOURITES**. MANAGER HUGO MEISL'S SIDE HAVE A GREAT **RECORD** - ONLY TWO DEFEATS IN THEIR LAST 30 MATCHES.

'Scoring a goal in Milan's San Siro is like winning a place in a woman's heart, only better' - Nicola Berti, Inter Milan and Italy

BUT THE **CONDITIONS** ARE TO PLAY A PART. THE AUSTRIANS' DELICATE SHORT PASSING GAME GETS **BOGGED DOWN** IN THE MUD.

AND ITALY'S ARGENTINIAN-BORN WINGER GUAITA **SCRAMBLES** HOME THE SEMI-FINAL'S ONLY GOAL.

CZECHOSLOVAKIA, PLAYING ATTRACTIVE FOOTBALL, ARE ALSO THROUGH TO THE FINAL AFTER **DISPOSING** OF GERMANY IN THE SEMIS. BEFORE THE MATCH THEY **PROUDLY** CARRY THEIR FLAG WHILE THE ITALIANS GIVE A FASCIST SALUTE.

UNUSUALLY, BOTH SIDES ARE CAPTAINED BY THEIR **GOALKEEPERS** - COMBI OF ITALY AND PLANICKA OF CZECHOSLOVAKIA.

THE CZECHS REFUSE TO BE INTIMIDATED BY THE **PARTISAN** ROMAN CROWD AND WHEN PUC SCORES FOLLOWING A 70TH-MINUTE CORNER THEY LOOK TO BE **HEADING** FOR VICTORY...

BUT THEY MISS TWO GREAT **CHANCES** TO TIE IT UP AND ORSI RESCUES ITALY WITH A BIZARRE **SWERVING** SHOT. THE MATCH GOES INTO EXTRA TIME.

AS LEGS BECOME **WEARY,** ITALY'S CENTRE-FORWARD ANGELO SCHIAVIO SUMMONS UP HIS LAST **RESERVE** OF STRENGTH TO HIT A DRAMATIC WINNER.

THE ITALIANS HAVE THE WORLD CUP AND A **DELIGHTED** MUSSOLINI HAS THE PROPAGANDA BOOST HE SO **DESPERATELY** WANTED.

'International sport is war without shooting' - George Orwell

First Round

Italy	7	USA	1	
Spain	3	Brazil	1	
Hungary	4	Egypt	2	
Austria	3	France	2	(aet)
Germany	5	Belgium	2	
Sweden	3	Argentina	2	
Switzerland	3	Holland	2	
Czechoslovakia	2	Romania	1	

Second Round

Italy	1	Spain	0
(after 1-1 draw)			
Austria	2	Hungary	1
Germany	2	Sweden	1
Czechoslovakia	3	Switzerland	2

aet = after extra-time

Semi-finals

Italy	1	Austria	0
Czechoslovakia	3	Germany	1

Third place play-off

Germany	3	Austria	2

Final

Italy	2	Czechoslovakia	1	(aet)

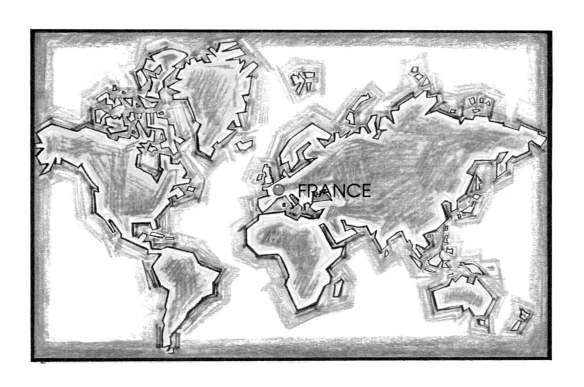

FRANCE

1938 FRANCE

FRANCE IS **PREFERRED** TO ARGENTINA AS THE VENUE FOR THE 1938 COMPETITION. IT'S THE PERFECT **SETTING** FOR THE WORLD'S TOP PLAYERS TO DISPLAY THEIR **FOOTBALLING** ARTISTRY.

AFTER **POLITICAL** CHANGES, THE GERMAN TEAM NOW INCLUDES THE BEST **AUSTRIAN** PLAYERS. BUT THEY ARE SURPRISE EARLY **CASUALTIES** - GOING DOWN 4-2 TO SWITZERLAND IN A REPLAY.

DEFENDING CHAMPIONS ITALY ALMOST FALL AT THE FIRST HURDLE. THEY **SCRAPE** AN EXTRA-TIME WIN OVER PLUCKY NORWAY WHO HAVE A GOAL **DISALLOWED** WHEN LEADING 1-0.

IN ANOTHER SHOCK, EXOTIC **NEWCOMERS** CUBA STUN KING CAROL'S ROMANIANS WITH A 2-1 **WIN** AFTER THE TEAMS HAD DRAWN 3-3.

UNDISPUTED MATCH OF THE TOURNAMENT IS THE BRAZIL-POLAND CLASH IN STRASBOURG. THIS GAME PROVIDES A **FEAST** OF GOALS.

BRAZIL'S 'BLACK DIAMOND' LEONIDAS DA SILVA BECOMES **ENTWINED** IN A PERSONAL SCORING DUEL WITH THE POWERFUL POLISH FORWARD WILLIMOWSKI - THEY **EACH** NOTCH FOUR.

IN THE END, **BRAZIL** TRIUMPH 6-5.

INCREDIBLY, THE TEAMS SHOW 15 **CHANGES** FOR THE REPLAY WHICH BRAZIL WIN 2-1.

UNFORTUNATELY, THE SOUTH AMERICANS' NEXT MATCH, AGAINST CZECHOSLOVAKIA, MAKES **HEADLINES** FOR THE WRONG REASONS. THREE PLAYERS ARE **SENT OFF** WHILE SEVERAL OTHERS ARE **INJURED** INCLUDING GOALIE PLANICKA.

14

'Football is all very well for rough girls, but it's hardly suitable for delicate boys' - Oscar Wilde

IN ANOTHER QUARTER-FINAL TIE, THE HOLDERS **KNOCK OUT** THE HOSTS. PIOLA NETS TWICE TO TAKE THE BLACK-SHIRTED ITALIANS **THROUGH** TO MEET BRAZIL.

FOR THE MARSEILLE SEMI-FINAL, BRAZIL **MISCALCULATE** AND LEAVE OUT LEONIDAS. THEIR ATTACK IS SUBSEQUENTLY **UNDERPOWERED** AND A MEAZZA PENALTY GIVES ITALY A 2-1 TRIUMPH.

IN THE OTHER SEMI-FINAL, **SWEDEN'S** 'TEAM OF STEEL' SHOCK HUNGARY WITH A **35 SECOND** OPENER FROM NYBERG.

BUT THE 'MAGYARS' HIT **BACK** WITH **FIVE** GOALS TO REACH THE FINAL.

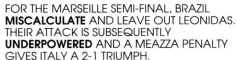

THE PARIS CROWD ANTICIPATES AN **INTRIGUING** CLASH OF STYLES - ITALY'S ENERGY AND SPEED AGAINST THE BALL-PLAYING **PRECISION** OF THE HUNGARIANS.

IN A **FLYING START**, COLAUSSI SHOOTS HOME TO PUT THE *AZZURRI* AHEAD....

...ONLY FOR TITKOS TO **EQUALISE** SIXTY SECONDS LATER.

BUT HUNGARY ALLOW THE **INSPIRATIONAL** MEAZZA TOO MUCH ROOM AND HE SETS UP FURTHER GOALS FOR PIOLA AND COLAUSSI. ITALY **LEAD** 3-1 AT HALF-TIME.

IN THE SECOND PERIOD, THE ITALIANS **SHUT UP** SHOP AND ALTHOUGH SAROSI PULLS ONE BACK, PIOLA'S **SHOT** CLINCHES IT AT 4-2.

MEAZZA BECOMES THE **SECOND** ITALIAN CAPTAIN TO COLLECT THE TROPHY BUT SADLY FOOTBALL IS SOON TO TAKE A **BACK SEAT** AS FIFA'S FAMILY OF NATIONS IS **TORN APART** BY WAR.

'All I know about the morality of men, I owe to football' - French philosopher Albert Camus

First Round

France	3	Belgium	1	
Italy	2	Norway	1	(aet)
Brazil	6	Poland	5	(aet)
Czechoslovakia	3	Holland	0	(aet)
Hungary	6	Dutch East Indies	0	
Cuba	2	Romania	1	
(after 3-3 draw)				
Switzerland	4	Germany	2	
(after 1-1 draw)				

(Sweden received bye)

Second Round

France	1	Italy	3
Brazil	2	Czechoslovakia	1
(after 1-1 draw)			
Sweden	8	Cuba	0
Hungary	2	Switzerland	0

Semi-finals

Italy	2	Brazil	1
Hungary	5	Sweden	1

Third place play-off

Brazil	4	Sweden	2

Final

Italy	4	Hungary	2

Vittorio Pozzo has a unique place in World Cup history as the only man to have managed two championship-winning teams.

The man who steered Italy to victory in 1934 and 1938 is remembered as a great student of the game who was, in many ways, remarkably ahead of his time.

Pozzo developed much of his tactical acumen in England where he regularly watched Manchester United's pre-World War I side.

He became a great admirer of United's style of play, in particular the long raking passes deployed by their centre-half Charlie Roberts.

When Pozzo was given charge of the Italian national team in 1929, he put to use all the knowledge he had gained from his friendships with footballing people such as Roberts and the respected Austrian coach Hugo Meisl.

He paid scrupulous attention to detail, going as far as to compile dossiers on all of Italy's opponents.

However, Pozzo could also be a strict disciplinarian and he was not slow to exploit the bombastic nationalism of the times for his own purposes.

Such was the case with the Argentinian-born players whom he selected on the grounds that they were liable for Italian military service.

'If they can die for Italy, they can play for Italy!' Pozzo maintained.

Enrique Guaita, a member of the 1934 World Cup winning side, was not so convinced.

When the Abyssinian War broke out in 1936, Guaita was caught trying to sneak across the border into Switzerland!

● Rome's PNF Stadium, where Pozzo's Italy completed their first World Cup triumph in 1934, was **demolished** in 1957. The Azteca Stadium in Mexico City is the only ground to have staged the World Cup Final twice.

● A **world-record** crowd of 199,854 watched the 1950 Brazil v Uruguay World Cup decider in Rio's Maracana Stadium. The 1950 tournament can also still boast the highest **average** attendance – 60,772 per match.

● The **lowest** crowd at a World Cup finals match was the 300 who witnessed Romania beat Peru in 1930. With the game being played on a Uruguayan public holiday the Montevideo public obviously found better things to occupy them.

● In 1973, the Soviet Union **pulled out** of the World Cup after refusing to play a qualifying match in Santiago's National Stadium. The Soviets were unhappy that Chile's anti-Communist regime had used the ground for the torture and execution of left-wing prisoners.

● The Toluca Stadium in Mexico which hosted matches in both the 1970 and 1986 World Cups is affectionately known as 'La Bombonera' or **'Chocolate Box'** after a box-like stand which was formerly at the ground. At 8,712 feet above sea-level, it's also the highest venue ever used for World Cup football.

● As well as Wembley, one other London venue was used in the 1966 tournament. However, it was not Arsenal's famous Highbury Stadium or Tottenham's White Hart Lane but the **greyhound racing** stadium White City. It staged the France v Uruguay group match because, ironically, Wembley was holding a greyhound meeting that evening.

● In July 1989, FIFA decreed that, from 1992 onwards, all World Cup matches would have to be played in **all-seater** stadia. Switzerland's bid to host the 1998 finals was thrown out because of their plans to use temporary stands.

● History will be made in the 1994 tournament when the Pontiac Silverdome, near Detroit, will stage the first-ever **indoor** World Cup finals matches. The playing surface will however be natural turf – a blend of ryegrass and Kentucky bluegrass, grown in California and transported to the Silverdome prior to the tournament.

● In 1979, Milan's magnificent San Siro ground was renamed the **Giuseppe Meazza Stadium** – in honour of Italy's 1938 World Cup-winning skipper. Meazza had been a popular player with both Inter and AC Milan.

● Playing in Gelsenkirchen's Parkstadion proved an uplifting experience for teams during the 1974 World Cup. Because the pitch is sunk some way below ground level, an **escalator** conveyed the players down from their dressing-rooms to the field and back up again. Just the job for those tired legs!

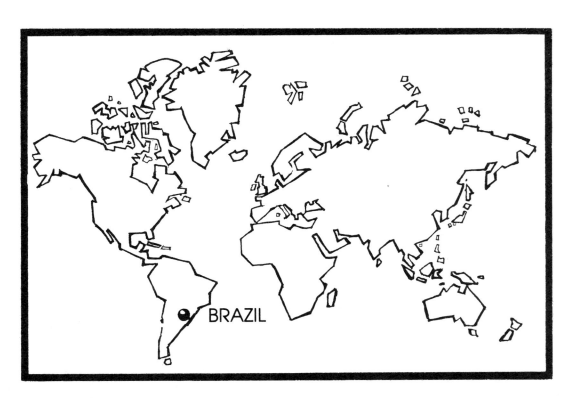

BRAZIL

1950 BRAZIL

1950 AND THE STORY **RECOMMENCES** IN BRAZIL WHERE FOOTBALL HAS REMAINED UNAFFECTED BY THE RAVAGES OF WAR. RIO PREPARES TO HOST AN **EXTRAVAGANT** SOCCER CARNIVAL.

JUSTIFYING THEIR POSITION AS **FAVOURITES**, THE HOSTS SLAM FOUR GOALS PAST **LUCKLESS** MEXICAN GOALKEEPER CARBAJAL.

IN THE MAGNIFICENT, BUT AS YET **UNFINISHED**, MARACANA STADIUM, A 21-GUN SALUTE GREETS THE BRAZILIAN TEAM AS THEY TAKE THE FIELD FOR THEIR **OPENING** POOL 1 MATCH.

AMONG THE **DIMINISHED** EUROPEAN REPRESENTATION, YUGOSLAVIA LOOK **STRONG** AS THEY STROLL TO VICTORIES OVER SWITZERLAND AND MEXICO.

BUT THE YUGOSLAVS BECOME JADED BY THE ILL-CONCEIVED **TRAVEL** ITINERARY AND BRAZIL EDGE THEM OUT IN THE POOL DECIDER IN RIO. ZIZINHO CLINCHES IT WITH A **SPLENDID** SOLO EFFORT.

MEANWHILE, ENGLAND MAKE THEIR **LONG-AWAITED** WORLD CUP DEBUT AND, IN THEIR SECOND MATCH, ARE ON THE RECEIVING END OF THE COMPETITION'S **BIGGEST UPSET** SO FAR.

PART-TIME **USA** BEAT THEM 1-0.

HAITIAN-BORN JOE 'LARRY' GAETJENS IS CARRIED OFF AS A NATIONAL **HERO**. AFTER ANOTHER DEFEAT BY SPAIN, ENGLAND ARE **OUT**.

ITALIAN HOPES OF ANOTHER TITLE HAD EFFECTIVELY **PERISHED**, ALONG WITH EIGHT OF THEIR SQUAD, IN THE PREVIOUS YEAR'S TURIN AIR CRASH.

THEY LOSE 3-2 TO **OLYMPIC** CHAMPS SWEDEN.

'Ridiculous, can't we play them again tomorrow?' - England's Wilf Mannion after defeat by the USA

SWEDEN ARE ONE OF FOUR TEAMS WHO QUALIFY FOR A **FINAL POOL** BUT THEY ARE **WALLOPED** BY FREE-SCORING BRAZIL. ADEMIR HITS FOUR IN THE **7-1** ROUT.

URUGUAY ARE THE ONLY **THREAT** TO BRAZIL AND IT TURNS OUT THAT THE MEETING OF THE TWO TEAMS WILL **DECIDE** THE WINNERS. A HUGE, **EXPECTANT** CROWD SQUEEZES INTO THE NOW-COMPLETED MARACANA.

THE BRAZILIANS NEED ONLY A **DRAW** TO TAKE THE TROPHY BUT THEY ARE NOT EVEN **CONTEMPLATING** THE POSSIBILITY OF DEFEAT. A SONG 'BRAZIL THE VICTORS' HAS **ALREADY** BEEN COMPOSED.

IN A **SUPERCHARGED** ATMOSPHERE, THE URUGUAYANS DEFEND SOLIDLY FOR THE FIRST HALF. BUT TWO MINUTES AFTER THE RESTART, FRIACA **SLIPS** THE HOME TEAM AHEAD.

NAIVELY, BRAZIL CONTINUE TO PRESS - LEAVING **GAPS** AT THE BACK. IN 66 MINUTES SHIAFFINO KNOCKS HOME AN EQUALISER.

URUGUAY ARE **LIFTED** BY THE GOAL .THEN, WITH 11 MINUTES LEFT, THE SAMBAS ARE **SILENCED** AS GHIGGIA THREADS IN A SENSATIONAL WINNER.

THE **UNTHINKABLE** HAS HAPPENED - URUGUAY HAVE COMPLETED THE ULTIMATE SOCCER **SMASH AND GRAB.** 'BRAZIL THE VICTORS' IS NEVER PLAYED AND A NATION GOES INTO **MOURNING.**

IN THE STATE OF MINAS GERAIS, A YOUNG BOY PROMISES HIS **DISTRAUGHT** DAD: "DON'T WORRY, FATHER, I'LL WIN THE CUP FOR YOU!". HIS NAME IS **EDSON** - BUT HE WILL EVENTUALLY BECOME KNOWN BY **ANOTHER** NAME - PELE

'The loser now will be later to win' - Bob Dylan

Pool 1

	P	W	D	L	F	A	Pts
Brazil	3	2	1	0	8	2	5
Yugoslavia	3	2	0	1	7	3	4
Switzerland	3	1	1	1	4	6	3
Mexico	3	0	0	3	2	10	0

Pool 2

	P	W	D	L	F	A	Pts
Spain	3	3	0	0	6	1	6
England	3	1	0	2	2	2	2
Chile	3	1	0	2	5	6	2
USA	3	1	0	2	4	8	2

Pool 3

	P	W	D	L	F	A	Pts
Sweden	2	1	1	0	5	4	3
Italy	2	1	0	1	4	3	2
Paraguay	2	0	1	1	2	4	1

Pool 4

Uruguay	8	Bolivia	0

Final Pool

Brazil	7	Sweden	1
Spain	2	Uruguay	2
Brazil	6	Spain	1
Uruguay	3	Sweden	2
Sweden	3	Spain	1
Brazil	1	Uruguay	2

Final Table

	P	W	D	L	F	A	Pts
Uruguay	3	2	1	0	7	5	5
Brazil	3	2	0	1	14	4	4
Sweden	3	1	0	2	6	11	2
Spain	3	0	1	2	4	11	1

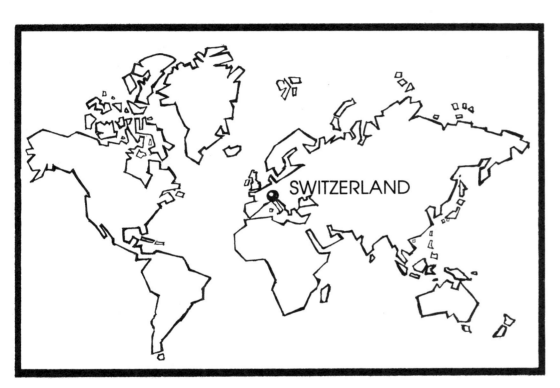

SWITZERLAND

1954 SWITZERLAND

IT'S 1954 AND THE **WORLD CUP** RETURNS TO EUROPE. SWITZERLAND, HOME OF FIFA, IS AN **APPROPRIATE** CHOICE OF VENUE.

HUNGARY ARE A SIDE **LITTERED** WITH TALENT - FROM THE 'GALLOPING MAJOR' FERENC PUSKAS TO THE **'GOLDEN HEAD'** SANDOR KOCSIS. MANY BELIEVE THE OUTCOME OF THE TOURNAMENT IS A **FOREGONE** CONCLUSION.

THE TEAM OF THE **MOMENT** IS HUNGARY. THE MAGYARS' RECORD IS EXCEPTIONAL - 27 GAMES **UNDEFEATED** - THEIR MOST FAMOUS RESULT BEING A 6-3 **DRUBBING** OF ENGLAND AT WEMBLEY.

THE HUNGARIANS' FIRST MATCH PRODUCES AN **OMINOUS** SCORELINE FOR THE REST. THEY **ANNIHILATE** SOUTH KOREA 9-0.

AFTER **MISSING OUT** IN 1950, GERMANY ARE BACK IN THE WORLD CUP - NOW AS WEST GERMANY. THEY **CELEBRATE** THEIR RETURN BY ROMPING TO A 4-1 VICTORY OVER TURKEY.

CUNNING GERMAN BOSS SEPP HERBERGER THEN **DELIBERATELY** FIELDS AN UNDERSTRENGTH TEAM AGAINST HUNGARY - **GAMBLING** THAT HIS SIDE CAN BEAT TURKEY AGAIN IN A **PLAY-OFF**.

HUNGARY WIN 8-3 BUT HERBERGER'S PLAN WORKS OUT.

THE SERIES IS PRODUCING A REAL **GOALS BONANZA.** IN THE QUARTER-FINALS, AUSTRIA DEFEAT SWITZERLAND **7-5** IN SUN-BAKED LAUSANNE.

THE HUNGARY-BRAZIL QUARTER-FINAL **UNEXPECTEDLY** TURNS INTO ONE OF THE MOST **SHAMEFUL** EPISODES IN WORLD CUP HISTORY. IT STARTS BRIGHTLY ENOUGH WHEN THE MAGYARS **RACE** INTO A TWO GOAL LEAD.

'The Hungarians have achieved a mastery over a football as great as any team in history' - Geoffrey Green, journalist, 1954

A **PENALTY** THEN LETS BRAZIL BACK INTO THE MATCH BUT, AS THE TENSION MOUNTS, THE TACKLING BECOMES **X-CERTIFICATE**. THREE PLAYERS ARE SENT OFF FOR VIOLENT CONDUCT.

HUNGARY HOLD OUT FOR A 4-2 VICTORY BUT THE **HOSTILITY** CONTINUES ON THE WAY TO THE DRESSING-ROOMS. NOT SURPRISINGLY, THE MATCH IS **DUBBED** 'THE BATTLE OF BERNE'.

FORTUNATELY, THE MAGYARS' SEMI-FINAL AGAINST URUGUAY PROVES AN ALTOGETHER **FINER** FOOTBALLING OCCASION. WITH DARKNESS FALLING, KOCSIS **NODS** HUNGARY THROUGH IN AN EXTRA-TIME THRILLER.

UNSEEDED WEST GERMANY ARE **ALSO** IN THE FINAL AFTER CONQUERING **NEIGHBOURS** AUSTRIA. HUNGARY BEAT THE GERMANS 8-3 IN THE POOL MATCH - SURELY THEY'LL WIN AGAIN IN **RAIN-SOAKED** BERNE?

IN A **WHIRLWIND** OPENING SPELL, SHORT-RANGE GOALS FROM PUSKAS AND CZIBOR HAVE HUNGARY TWO **IN FRONT**. AFTER ONLY EIGHT MINUTES, IT LOOKS **CUT AND DRIED** FOR THE MAGYARS.

BUT THE DREADED ENEMY **COMPLACENCY** CREEPS IN. MORLOCK REDUCES THE **ARREARS** THEN RAHN VOLLEYS AN EQUALISER FROM A CORNER.

HUNGARY STIR AGAIN BUT, WITH PUSKAS INJURED, THEY ARE **SHORT** OF THEIR BEST. AS EXTRA-TIME LOOMS, RAHN **ARROWS** HOME THE CLINCHER FOR WEST GERMANY.

ONCE AGAIN, THE FINAL SCRIPT HAS BEEN DRAMATICALLY **RE-WRITTEN**, HUNGARY'S 27 GOALS IN THE TOURNAMENT COUNT FOR LITTLE AS HERBERGER'S **UNDERDOGS** TAKE THE VICTORY SPOILS.

'There is no such thing as second place. Either you're first or you're nothing!' - George Weiss, New York Yankees executive

Pool 1

	P	W	D	L	F	A	Pts
Brazil	2	1	1	0	6	1	3
Yugoslavia	2	1	1	0	2	1	3
France	2	1	0	1	3	3	2
Mexico	2	0	0	2	2	8	0

Pool 2

	P	W	D	L	F	A	Pts
Hungary	2	2	0	0	17	3	4
Turkey	2	1	0	1	8	4	2
West Germany	2	1	0	1	7	9	2
South Korea	2	0	0	2	0	16	0

Play-off
West Germany 7 Turkey 2

Pool 3

	P	W	D	L	F	A	Pts
Uruguay	2	2	0	0	9	0	4
Austria	2	2	0	0	6	0	4
Czechoslovakia	2	0	0	2	0	7	0
Scotland	2	0	0	2	0	8	0

Pool 4

	P	W	D	L	F	A	Pts
England	2	1	1	0	6	4	3
Italy	2	1	0	1	5	3	2
Switzerland	2	1	0	1	2	3	2
Belgium	2	0	1	1	5	8	1

Play-off
Switzerland 4 Italy 1

Quarter-finals

Austria	7	Switzerland	5
Uruguay	4	England	2
Hungary	4	Brazil	2
West Germany	2	Yugoslavia	0

Semi-finals

West Germany	6	Austria	1
Hungary	4	Uruguay	2 (*aef*)

Third place play-off

Austria	3	Uruguay	1

Final

West Germany	3	Hungary	2

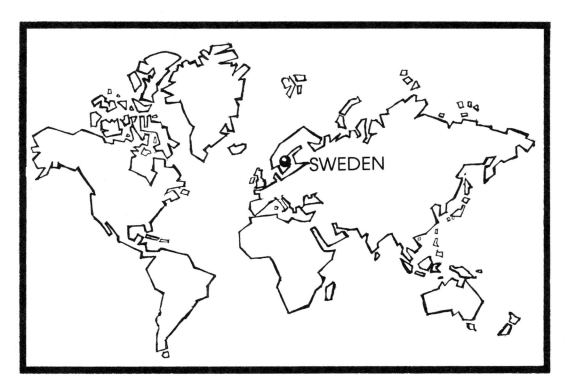

SWEDEN

1958 SWEDEN

AS FIFA'S MEMBERSHIP **EXPANDS**, THE 1958 WORLD CUP BECOMES THE MOST **REPRESENTATIVE** COMPETITION YET. HOWEVER, IT'S ANOTHER EUROPEAN COUNTRY, SWEDEN, WHICH **WELCOMES** THE WORLD'S TOP FOOTBALLERS.

FOR THE FIRST AND **ONLY** TIME, ALL FOUR **BRITISH** TEAMS REACH THE FINALS. 'NO-HOPERS' NORTHERN IRELAND ENJOY A FIRST-ROUND **PLAY-OFF** VICTORY OVER CZECHOSLOVAKIA.

IN STOCKHOLM, **WALES** PIP A HUNGARY SIDE SADLY DEPLETED BY **DEFECTIONS** FOLLOWING THE 1956 UPRISING.

MEANWHILE, WORLD CUP **NEWCOMERS** SOVIET UNION COME UP AGAINST ANOTHER DEBUTANT IN THEIR POOL MATCH AGAINST BRAZIL - **17-YEAR-OLD** PELE.

THE BRAZILIANS, DEPLOYING THE **INNOVATIVE** 4-2-4 TACTICAL FORMATION ISSUE A WARNING TO THE OTHERS WITH A **CONVINCING** 2-0 WIN.

IN THE QUARTER-FINALS, THE MINNOWS' **FAIRYTALE** ENDS. A BATTLE-WEARY NORTHERN IRELAND DEFENCE HAS **NO ANSWER** TO THE FLAMBOYANT FRENCH FORWARDS.

BUT WALES **COME CLOSE** TO PULLING OFF A SHOCK. THEY HOLD BRAZIL FOR 73 MINUTES BEFORE BEING K.O.'D BY **PELE'S** FIRST-EVER WORLD CUP GOAL.

SURPRISINGLY, SWEDISH FANS HAD BEEN **SLOW** TO RESPOND TO THEIR OWN TEAM'S PROGRESS - UNTIL THE SEMI-FINAL IN GOTHENBURG. EGGED ON BY **CHEERLEADERS**, THE CROWD SPUR SWEDEN TO A 3-1 VICTORY OVER GERMANY.

It's our new tactics - we equalise before the others have scored!' - Northern Ireland's Danny Blanchflower

IN STOCKHOLM, A **MOUTH-WATERING** MATCH SEES BRAZIL BOOK THEIR FINAL BERTH WITH A 5-2 TRIUMPH OVER FRANCE. PELE **HITS** A HAT-TRICK.

FOR THE FRENCH, A 6-3 WIN IN THE **THIRD PLACE** PLAY-OFF PROVIDES SOME CONSOLATION - AS DOES THE **RECORD-BREAKING** 13-GOAL HAUL OF THEIR STRIKER JUSTE FONTAINE.

BEFORE THE FINAL, IT RAINS **SOLIDLY** FOR 24 HOURS. THE HEAVY PITCH COULD PROVE AN **ADVANTAGE** FOR SWEDEN.

IN **FOUR** MINUTES, THE HOME TEAM ARE AHEAD. LIEDHOLM CARVES OUT AN OPENING AND HIS SHOT **ELUDES** 'KEEPER GYLMAR.

BUT THE SWEDES' JOY IS **SHORT-LIVED**. FIVE MINUTES LATER, GARRINCHA SCUTTLES DOWN THE WING AND **CROSSES** FOR VAVA TO SCORE. AFTER HALF-AN-HOUR, A **CARBON-COPY** MOVE HAS THE BLUE-SHIRTED BRAZILIANS 2-1 IN FRONT.

THE **SECOND HALF** BELONGS TO PELE. IN 55 MINUTES, THE BOY WONDER **CONJURES** UP A PIECE OF MAGIC. HE DEFTLY FLICKS THE BALL OVER HIS OPPONENT'S HEAD BEFORE **VOLLEYING** HOME BRAZIL'S THIRD.

THEN, AFTER EACH SIDE HAD SCORED AGAIN, PELE **CAPS** A SENSATIONAL TOURNAMENT WITH A **LOOPING** HEADER TO MAKE IT 5-2.

BRAZIL ARE VICTORIOUS **AT LAST** - BECOMING THE FIRST TEAM TO WIN THE CUP OUTSIDE OF THEIR **OWN CONTINENT**. THE NEW CHAMPIONS SPORTINGLY CARRY A HUGE **SWEDISH** FLAG AROUND THE PITCH. IT'S BEEN A **MEMORABLE** DAY FOR FOOTBALL.

'Brazilian football comes from the heart' - Pele

Pool 1

	P	W	D	L	F	A	Pts
West Germany	3	1	2	0	7	5	4
Northern Ireland	3	1	1	1	4	5	3
Czechoslovakia	3	1	1	1	8	4	3
Argentina	3	1	0	2	5	10	2

Play-off

Northern Ireland	2	Czechoslovakia	1	(aef)

Pool 2

	P	W	D	L	F	A	Pts
France	3	2	0	1	11	7	4
Yugoslavia	3	1	2	0	7	6	4
Paraguay	3	1	1	1	9	12	3
Scotland	3	0	1	2	4	6	1

Pool 3

	P	W	D	L	F	A	Pts
Sweden	3	2	1	0	5	1	5
Hungary	3	1	1	1	6	3	3
Wales	3	0	3	0	2	2	3
Mexico	3	0	1	2	1	8	1

Play-off

Wales	2	Hungary	1

Pool 4

	P	W	D	L	F	A	Pts
Brazil	3	2	1	0	5	0	5
England	3	0	3	0	4	4	3
USSR	3	1	1	1	4	4	3
Austria	3	0	1	2	2	7	1

Play-off

USSR	1	England	0

Quarter-finals

Brazil	1	Wales	0
France	4	Northern Ireland	0
West Germany	1	Yugoslavia	0
Sweden	2	USSR	0

Semi-finals

Brazil	5	France	2
Sweden	3	West Germany	1

Third place play-off

France	6	West Germany	3

Final

Brazil	5	Sweden	2

CHILE

1962 CHILE

SURPRISINGLY, **EARTHQUAKE-HIT** CHILE IS ACCORDED THE 1962 TOURNAMENT - THANKS LARGELY TO THE EFFORTS OF THEIR FA PRESIDENT CARLOS **DITTBORN**. SADLY, HE DOESN'T LIVE TO SEE THE OPENING CEREMONY IN SANTIAGO.

WITH THE SNOW-CAPPED ANDES PROVIDING A **SPECTACULAR** BACKDROP, THE HOST NATION MAKE A BRIGHT **START** BY BEATING SWITZERLAND 3-1.

BRAZIL, PRACTICALLY **UNCHANGED** FROM 1958, ARE STRONGLY FANCIED TO WIN AGAIN BUT THEY SUFFER A **BLOW** WHEN PELE HOBBLES OUT OF THE TOURNAMENT DURING THE MATCH AGAINST CZECHOSLOVAKIA.

IN THEIR NEXT GAME, THE BRAZILIANS ENCOUNTER A **FAMOUS** WORLD CUP FIGURE. HUNGARIAN EXILE FERENC PUSKAS NOW WEARS THE **COLOURS** OF SPAIN.

BACK IN GROUP TWO - A POTENTIAL **FLASHPOINT** EMERGES BETWEEN CHILE AND ITALY WHOSE JOURNALISTS HAVE INSENSITIVELY SLATED THE HOST COUNTRY. IT ISN'T LONG BEFORE THE **RESENTMENT** BOILS OVER.

IN WHAT BECOMES KNOWN AS 'THE BATTLE OF SANTIAGO', ITALY HAVE **TWO PLAYERS** DISMISSED WHILE CHILEAN SANCHEZ AMAZINGLY **STAYS ON** DESPITE BREAKING AN OPPONENT'S NOSE! CHILE WIN 2-0.

AFTER A RATHER **DISAPPOINTING** OPENING PHASE, THE QUARTER-FINALS PAIR CHILE WITH THE SOVIET UNION. A **NIGHTMARE** DISPLAY BY THE NORMALLY-RELIABLE RUSSIAN **GOALIE** YASHIN LETS THE HOME TEAM GO THROUGH.

ALSO IN THE LAST EIGHT, **ENGLAND** GIVE BRAZIL A RUN FOR THEIR MONEY BEFORE **SUCCUMBING** TO THE HOLDERS' SUPERIOR SKILLS. GARRINCHA'S 'BANANA' SHOT SEALS IT.

'The 1958 and 1962 World Cups were garden parties compared to what is involved now' - West German manager Helmut Schoen, 1978

IN AN **ALL-SOUTH AMERICAN** SEMI, BRAZIL SCUPPER CHILE'S GRAND AMBITIONS. **THAT** MAN GARRINCHA SETS THEM ON THEIR WAY WITH A **VENOMOUS** 20-YARDER.

FOR **CHILEAN** FANS, THE REAL 'FINAL' IS THE THIRD PLACE MATCH BETWEEN **THEIR SIDE** AND THE YUGOSLAVS. THE HOSTS WIN 1-0.

BEFORE A **SPARSE** CROWD, DEFENCE-ORIENTATED CZECHOSLOVAKIA OVERCOME EASTERN BLOC **RIVALS** YUGOSLAVIA IN THE OTHER SEMI-FINAL.

THE ONE **BLIGHT** ON BRAZIL'S SEMI-FINAL TRIUMPH HAD BEEN GARRINCHA'S ORDERING-OFF. AFTER AN **ANXIOUS** 24-HOUR WAIT, FIFA PRESIDENT STANLEY ROUS **DECREES** THAT THE 'LITTLE BIRD' CAN PLAY IN THE FINAL.

ON THE DAY, IT'S THE **UNDERDOGS** WHO TAKE A SHOCK LEAD. SCHERER SPLITS THE BRAZILIAN DEFENCE AND MASOPUST **SLAMS** THE BALL PAST GYLMAR.

AFTER **ZITO** HAD HEADED BRAZIL IN FRONT, SCHROIFF MAKES ANOTHER **CRUCIAL** GAFF IN THE 77TH MINUTE. HE FUMBLES IN THE BRIGHT SUN **ALLOWING** VAVA TO TAP IN A DECISIVE THIRD GOAL.

BUT CZECH '**KEEPER** SCROIFF, A HERO IN EARLIER ROUNDS, TURNS **VILLAIN** AS HE ALLOWS AMARILDO'S SHOT TO **SWERVE** PAST HIM FOR THE EQUALISER.

SO BRAZIL **RETAIN** THEIR TITLE - ALBEIT IN A LESS EXHILARATING FASHION THAN IN '58. SKIPPER MAURO BECOMES THE **SEVENTH MAN** TO COLLECT THE RIMET TROPHY.

'Who would have expected Amarildo to curl a shot in from that position?' - Czech goalie Wilhelm Schroiff

Group 1

	P	W	D	L	F	A	Pts
USSR	3	2	1	0	8	5	5
Yugoslavia	3	2	0	1	8	3	4
Uruguay	3	1	0	2	4	6	2
Colombia	3	0	1	2	5	11	1

Group 2

	P	W	D	L	F	A	Pts
West Germany	3	2	1	0	4	1	5
Chile	3	2	0	1	5	3	4
Italy	3	1	1	1	3	2	3
Switzerland	3	0	0	3	2	8	0

Group 3

	P	W	D	L	F	A	Pts
Brazil	3	2	1	0	4	1	5
Czechoslovakia	3	1	1	1	2	3	3
Mexico	3	1	0	2	3	4	2
Spain	3	1	0	2	2	3	2

Group 4

	P	W	D	L	F	A	Pts
Hungary	3	2	1	0	8	2	5
England	3	1	1	1	4	3	3
Argentina	3	1	1	1	2	3	3
Bulgaria	3	0	1	2	1	7	1

Quarter-finals

Brazil	3	England	1
Chile	2	USSR	1
Yugoslavia	1	West Germany	0
Czechoslovakia	1	Hungary	0

Semi-finals

Brazil	4	Chile	2
Czechoslovakia	3	Yugoslavia	1

Third place play-off

Chile	1	Yugoslavia	0

Final

Brazil	3	Czechoslovakia	1

To this day, **Sepp Herberger**, manager of West Germany's 1954 World Cup winning team, is regarded as one of the giant figures of German football.

He is the man responsible for moulding the national side into a major force in the world game.

Although only a little man, Herberger is said to have enjoyed an incredible power over his players – one which inspired them to perform miracles of strength and stamina.

The former Mannheim inside-forward was first given his chance as a coach after Germany's poor showing in the 1936 Berlin Olympics.

Immediately, his style of vigorous, personable management began to produce results and the Germans dropped just one point in 11 matches.

But it was in the 1954 World Cup finals that Herberger showed the full extent of his tactical cunning.

He let his team virtually throw a group match against Hungary in the assured knowledge that they would win a play-off against Turkey and thus embark on an easier route to the Final.

West Germany's Final victory over the fabled Hungarians ranks not only as one of the biggest World Cup surprises to date but as a remarkable triumph for Herberger's shrewd management.

Herberger also led West Germany in the 1958 and 1962 tournaments, taking them to fourth place and the quarter-finals respectively.

When he abdicated in favour of his protege, Helmut Schoen, in 1964, he left a side well-placed to challenge for honours.

Herberger died, at the age of 80, in 1977.

● The World Cup was **first** televised in 1954 although coverage was modest by today's standards. For Scottish viewers, the first-ever 'live' World Cup tie to feature their team turned into a real horror show – the Dark Blues crashed **7-0** to Uruguay in Basle.

● Nowadays television is a crucial part of any World Cup tournament since it's the guarantee of **global exposure** which persuades companies to invest in the event. For the 1994 World Cup, FIFA sold official sponsorship packages for $15-20 million each.

● In the late 1980s, FIFA flirted with the idea of playing a match in **four quarters** instead of two halves to allow more opportunities for commercials to be shown. Although this was rejected, viewers of the 1994 tournament can expect to see sponsors' logos super-imposed on the screen during matches.

● The 1966 tournament was the first World Cup to receive major TV coverage by way of satellite. Probably the most famous World Cup **commentary** lines ever uttered came from BBC's Kenneth Wolstenholme at

the '66 Final. As Geoff Hurst ran through to score England's fourth goal, Wolstenholme quipped: 'Some people are on the pitch, they think it's all over .... it is now!'.

● In 1970 and 1986, the timing of matches in Mexico was arranged to suit television coverage **in Europe**. Many of the games kicked off at noon – when it's not even advisable to walk about – never mind play football.

● Before the 1978 World Cup, Argentina's military government ran **TV commercials** which urged people to be on their best behaviour during the tournament. They were anxious that the 'sunny side' of Argentinian life should be presented to all the foreign visitors.

● The Brazil-England clash in the 1970 tournament was seen by 32.5 million people in Britain – second only to the 1981 **Royal Wedding** in the UK's all-time audience ratings. The 1970 finals were the first to be screened in colour.

● Peru's 1982 centre-forward Guillermo La Rosa had been brought home from club football in Colombia by **cash** put up by a TV station. La

Rosa scored Peru's consolation goal in the 5-1 drubbing by Poland in La Coruna.

● More than one billion people watched the 1990 World Cup Final 'live' on television, **triple** the audience that saw the moon-landing in 1969. It's estimated that half the world's population viewed at least one match of the *Italia '90* tournament.

● In 1974, Final referee Jack Taylor was under no illusions about television's role in **widening awareness** of the game. Said Taylor: 'Old ladies who've been coming into my butcher's shop for years have suddenly started talking about sweepers and making space!'

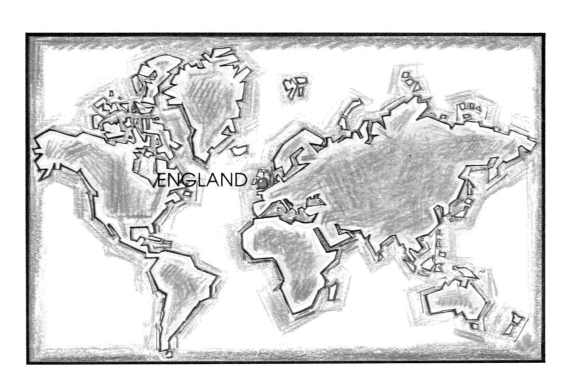

ENGLAND

1966 ENGLAND

THE 1966 TOURNAMENT IN ENGLAND THROWS UP AN **UNLIKELY** HERO - BEFORE A BALL IS EVEN KICKED. BLACK-AND-WHITE **MONGREL** 'PICKLES' FINDS THE RIMET TROPHY AFTER IT HAD BEEN **STOLEN** WHILE ON DISPLAY IN LONDON.

ON THE **FOOTBALLING** FRONT, ENGLAND MANAGER ALF RAMSEY THROWS ASIDE HIS USUAL CAUTION. 'WE WILL **WIN** THE WORLD CUP', HE **CONFIDENTLY** PREDICTS.

BUT THE **HOME TEAM'S** START IS UNINSPIRING. SHORT ON IDEAS, THEY ARE UNABLE TO **BREACH** AN OBSTINATE URUGUAY DEFENCE.

AFTER HALF-AN-HOUR OF THEIR **NEXT** MATCH AGAINST MEXICO, ENGLAND STILL HAVEN'T **FOUND THE NET**. BOBBY CHARLTON'S 30-YARD THUNDERBOLT LIFTS THE TENSION AND **SETS** RAMSEY'S MEN ON THEIR WAY.

DEFENDING CHAMPIONS BRAZIL FIND THEMSELVES IN A **TOUGH** GROUP. THEIR TOP STAR PELE IS INJURED AGAINST BULGARIA AND THEIR 12-YEAR UNBEATEN RECORD **FALLS** TO THE RESURGENT HUNGARIANS.

PELE **REAPPEARS** FOR BRAZIL'S CRUCIAL MATCH WITH PORTUGAL BUT HE IS SINGLED OUT FOR SOME **CRUDE** TREATMENT. AS HE LIMPS OFF, BRAZIL'S HOPES OF A CUP TREBLE TAKE A **NOSEDIVE**.

A **NEW STAR** IS EMERGING, MOZAMBIQUE-BORN EUSEBIO KILLS OFF BRAZIL WITH TWO PIECES OF **CLASS** FINISHING.

SADLY, **VIOLENT PLAY** IS BECOMING ALL TOO PREVALENT. WEST GERMANY ARE ON THE RECEIVING END OF SOME **CYNICAL** TACKLING FROM ARGENTINA WHO ARE WARNED BY FIFA ABOUT THEIR **AGGRESSIVE** APPROACH.

'It looks as though brutality pays' - Pele, 1966

BUT **PROVING** THAT FOOTBALL STILL HAS ITS ROMANTIC SIDE, LITTLE NORTH KOREA PULL OFF THE BIGGEST **SHOCK** SINCE 1950 WHEN THEY INFLICT AN IGNOMINIOUS DEFEAT ON **FORMER** WINNERS ITALY.

AND THE ASIAN SHOCK-TROOPS ARE **FAR** FROM FINISHED. IN THE QUARTER-FINAL, THEY **STORM** INTO A SENSATIONAL THREE-GOAL LEAD AGAINST PORTUGAL.

AMIDST THE **EUPHORIA** HOWEVER, THE KOREANS LEAVE THEIR BACK DOOR **UNLOCKED**. IN ONE OF THE MOST AMAZING COMEBACKS OF ALL TIME, EUSEBIO DELIVERS A FOUR-GOAL **SALVO** TO DESTROY THEIR DREAM.

ELSEWHERE, THE **DARKER SIDE** OF SOUTH AMERICAN SOCCER EMERGES AGAIN. TWO URUGUAYANS ARE **ORDERED OFF** IN THEIR LAST-EIGHT DEFEAT BY WEST GERMANY.

WHILE, AT WEMBLEY, **UNREPENTANT** ARGENTINA **INDULGE** IN FURTHER UNSAVOURY TACTICS AGAINST ENGLAND. THE REFEREE'S PATIENCE RUNS OUT AND THE **PETULANT** RATTIN IS SENT PACKING.

ENGLAND SURPRISINGLY **STRUGGLE** AGAINST TEN MEN AND IT'S LEFT TO NEWLY-INTRODUCED **STRIKER** GEOFF HURST TO BREAK THE DEADLOCK WITH AN EXCELLENT **GLANCING** HEADER.

AFTER THE FINAL WHISTLE, ALF RAMSEY, **INCENSED** BY ARGENTINA'S BEHAVIOUR, INTERVENES TO **PREVENT** THE CUSTOMARY SWAPPING OF JERSEYS. HE LATER **BRANDS** THE ARGENTINIANS 'ANIMALS'.

IN THE SEMI-FINALS, THE WEST GERMAN MACHINE **ROLLS ON**. A PILEDRIVER FROM THEIR YOUNG MIDFIELD STAR FRANZ BECKENBAUER **SIGNALS THE END** FOR THE SOVIET UNION.

'The Argentinians are no more dirty or less sporting than anyone else' - Alfredo di Stefano, former Argentina international

THE OTHER SEMI PROMISES AN INTRIGUING **PERSONAL** DUEL BETWEEN GRITTY ENGLAND MARKER NOBBY STILES AND THE **GIFTED** EUSEBIO. CAN THE 'TOOTHLESS TIGER' TAME THE 'BLACK PANTHER'?

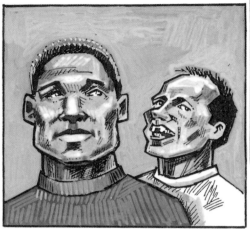

IN A **HIGHLY-SPORTING** CONTEST, EUSEBIO IS STRANGELY SUBDUED AND IT'S BOBBY CHARLTON WHO TAKES **CENTRE-STAGE**. IN THE 30TH MINUTE, HE POUNCES ON A REBOUND TO **SIDE-FOOT** THE OPENER.

11 MINUTES FROM TIME, CHARLTON'S BLISTERING SHOT **HUMS** PAST 'KEEPER PEREIRA TO GIVE ENGLAND WHAT LOOKS LIKE AN **UNASSAILABLE** LEAD.

ALTHOUGH HE **SCORES** A CONSOLATION PENALTY, EUSEBIO'S WORLD CUP IS OVER. HE **DEPARTS** THE WEMBLEY TURF IN TEARS.

FOR THE FINAL, ENGLAND ARE **MARGINAL** FAVOURITES BUT IT'S BEEN 32 YEARS SINCE A **HOST NATION** HAS WON THE TROPHY.

IN AN EDGY **OPENING** PERIOD, A GOAL ALWAYS LOOKS LIKELY. AN UNCHARACTER-ISTICALLY **SLOPPY** HEADER FROM ENGLAND FULL-BACK WILSON DROPS TO HALLER WHO GLEEFULLY **ACCEPTS** THE CHANCE.

WITHIN **SIX** MINUTES, ENGLAND ARE LEVEL. A QUICKLY-TAKEN FREE-KICK FROM CAPTAIN BOBBY MOORE **FINDS** HURST IN SPLENDID ISOLATION - 1-1.

GRADUALLY, ENGLAND GET **ON TOP** AND, IN 78 MINUTES, THEY TAKE A DESERVED LEAD. PETERS **PRODS** HOME A DEFLECTED SHOT AND THE CROWD PREPARES TO **PROCLAIM** VICTORY.

'I thought my goal was going to be the winner' - Martin Peters

BUT THERE IS A **STING** IN THE TAIL. IN THE FINAL MINUTE SWISS REFEREE DIENST **AWARDS** WEST GERMANY A CONTENTIOUS FREE-KICK IN A **DANGEROUS** POSITION.

EMMERICH SHOOTS AND, AS THE BALL **BOBBLES** AROUND THE ENGLAND BOX, DEFENDER WEBER POPS UP TO **SNATCH** A SENSATIONAL EQUALISER.

THE FINAL WHISTLE **BLOWS** - ENGLAND WERE JUST SECONDS FROM WINNING. BEFORE THE EXTRA-TIME, MANAGER RAMSEY **LIFTS** HIS DISAPPOINTED PLAYERS, TELLING THEM: 'YOU'VE WON IT **ONCE,** NOW DO IT AGAIN!'.

THERE'S PLENTY MORE **DRAMA** TO COME. TEN MINUTES AFTER THE RESTART, HURST **SMACKS** A SHOT AGAINST THE **UNDERSIDE** OF THE CROSSBAR. THE BALL BOUNCES DOWN AND **OUT** AGAIN.

ENGLAND CLAIM A GOAL BUT WAS THE **WHOLE BALL** OVER THE LINE? WEMBLEY HOLDS ITS BREATH AS HERR DIENST **CONSULTS** HIS LINESMAN.

THE SECONDS SEEM LIKE **MINUTES.** THEN SUDDENLY THE SWISS OFFICIAL POINTS TO THE **CENTRE-CIRCLE** AND THE HOME FANS ERUPT INTO DELIRIUM.

AS THE CLOCK TICKS **ROUND**, THE GERMANS GAMBLE EVERYTHING IN SEARCH OF **ANOTHER** EQUALISER. BUT HURST BREAKS CLEAR AND HE **LASHES** A LEFT-FOOT DRIVE PAST TILKOWSKI TO PUT THE ISSUE **BEYOND** ALL DOUBT.

DESPITE THE CONTROVERSY, ENGLAND ARE **GOOD VALUE** FOR THEIR VICTORY. HURST'S HAT-TRICK, THE **FIRST-EVER** IN A FINAL, HAS ENSURED THAT RAMSEY'S BOLD **PROPHECY** IS FULFILLED.

'It's only 12 inches high, solid gold - and it means England are the world champions' - BBC commentator Kenneth Wolstenholme

Group 1

	P	W	D	L	F	A	Pts
England	3	2	1	0	4	0	5
Uruguay	3	1	2	0	2	1	4
Mexico	3	0	2	1	1	3	2
France	3	0	1	2	2	5	1

Group 2

	P	W	D	L	F	A	Pts
West Germany	3	2	1	0	7	1	5
Argentina	3	2	1	0	4	1	5
Spain	3	1	0	2	4	5	2
Switzerland	3	0	0	3	1	9	0

Group 3

	P	W	D	L	F	A	Pts
Portugal	3	3	0	0	9	2	6
Hungary	3	2	0	1	7	5	4
Brazil	3	1	0	2	4	6	2
Bulgaria	3	0	0	3	1	8	0

Group 4

	P	W	D	L	F	A	Pts
USSR	3	3	0	0	6	1	6
North Korea	3	1	1	1	2	4	3
Italy	3	1	0	2	2	2	2
Chile	3	0	1	2	2	5	1

Quarter-finals

England	1	Argentina	0
Portugal	5	North Korea	3
USSR	2	Hungary	1
West Germany	4	Uruguay	0

Semi-finals

England	2	Portugal	1
West Germany	2	USSR	1

Third place play-off

Portugal	2	USSR	1

Final

England	4	West Germany	2 (aet)

Knighted by Queen Elizabeth after his team's World Cup victory, **Alf Ramsey** can claim to have been involved in both England's brightest and blackest footballing moments.

As a solid, ball-using right-back, he played in the England side which was embarrassingly beaten by the USA in the 1950 World Cup.

Although that reverse by no means overshadowed a creditable international playing career, it was as a manager that Ramsey was to reach new heights of achievement.

Between 1955 and 1962, he led unfashionable Ipswich Town from Third Division obscurity to the First Division Championship – an extraordinary feat.

When he was appointed as England's first true modern-style manager in 1963, Ramsey stuck to his policy of building a side based on work-rate and a strict playing pattern.

His early results were indifferent but, unmoved, he continued to direct his efforts towards the 1966 World Cup.

For the finals, Ramsey devised a novel 'no-wingers' tactical formation and successfully blended some good players and some modest individuals into a world-beating side.

And despite question-marks about his teams' lack of style, his 11-year reign must be regarded as England's most-fruitful period of modern times.

Sir Alf though, was never a media favourite and his public image as a cold and sombre man stemmed from a basic mistrust of the press.

The Ramsey era ended, rather meekly, in 1974 after England failed to negotiate the qualifying competition for that year's World Cup.

● Probably the biggest legacy of England's 1966 World Cup win was the establishment of the 4-3-3 tactical formation which dispensed with the traditional position of **winger**. With no real class wingers at his disposal, England manager Ramsey created a system which simply did not require them.

● In the early days of football, a team's line-up usually consisted of a goalkeeper, a three-quarter-back, a half-back and **eight forwards**. As it became clear that defences needed to be strengthened, Cambridge University were among the first teams to use two full-backs and three half-backs, in 1877.

● A big tactical watershed came in 1925, when the off-side law was made less strict. Many British teams adopted a  **'stopper'** centre-half to combat the glut in goalscoring. In Austria however,

'*Wunderteam*' coach Hugo Meisl retained the centre-half as an attacking position and it was a pivotal part of his successful short-passing game.

● It had been the Scots who had developed the art of **passing the ball** in order to make progress up the field. When the game of soccer first evolved, a player merely dribbled until he lost possession and hoped a team-mate was on hand to support him.

● In the 1930s, the midfield was recognised as the key strategic area and the **'WM' formation**, using deep-lying inside-forwards, was developed. In the 1950s, Hungary, and then particularly Brazil, evolved this into the **4-2-4** system.

● Surprisingly, the footballing philosophy of the 1960s seemed at odds with the carefree spirit of the times. The trend was towards more **defensive** formations such as 4-3-3 and 4-4-2 with the result that midfield areas became saturated and creative play stifled.

● In Italy, the notoriously-cautious coaches perfected the *catenaccio* or

'bolt' defensive system. This entailed a *libero* (a free-man or 'sweeper') who operated as a spare defender behind tight man-to-man marking. Later, West German star Franz Beckenbauer created the more positive role of **attacking** sweeper and exploited the freedom by driving forward and joining in attacks.

● A popular tactic nowadays is the the so-called '**pressing game**'whereby defenders push up towards the midfield. This has a dual effect – it protects their own goal by distance and also squeezes the space in which opponents can play.

● Undoubtedly, the most exciting tactics used in modern World Cup tournaments were those of Holland in 1974. Endowed with a highly-talented group of players, the Dutch team adopted the idealistic concept of **'Total Football'** where every player was a potential attacker or indeed defender. Interestingly, it was a philosophy which had first been propounded in 1955 by Willy Meisl, brother of Austrian manager Hugo.

MEXICO

1970 MEXICO

BECAUSE OF ITS **HEAT** AND ALTITUDE, MEXICO IS A SURPRISING CHOICE OF VENUE IN 1970. WILL THE FOOTBALLS FLY THROUGH THE **RAREFIED** AIR LIKE THE BALLOONS AT THE OPENING CEREMONY?

UNIQUELY, EL SALVADOR TAKE THEIR PLACE AFTER FIGHTING A **WAR** WITH A QUALIFYING GROUP OPPONENT. THEIR PLAY-OFF DEFEAT OF HONDURAS HAD **SPARKED OFF** A FIERCE THREE-DAY CONFLICT.

THERE ARE IMPORTANT I**NNOVATIONS** - THE USE OF SUBSTITUTES AND THE CARD **CAUTIONING** SYSTEM. THE YELLOW VERSION IS SHOWN TO FOUR SOVIET PLAYERS IN A TONE-SETTING **OPENER** AGAINST MEXICO.

LUCK IS NOT WITH THE SALVADORIANS. MEXICO SCORE FROM A QUICK FREE-KICK AND THE REFEREE **ALLOWS** THE GOAL - DESPITE HAVING AWARDED EL SALVADOR THE FOUL IN THE **FIRST** PLACE.

ELSEWHERE, CONCERNS ABOUT THE CONDITIONS APPEAR **UNFOUNDED** AS THE CONTESTANTS SERVE UP SOME GREAT FOOTBALL AND **PLENTY** OF GOALS. WEST GERMANY'S GERD MÜLLER HITS **HAT-TRICKS** AGAINST BULGARIA AND PERU.

GROUP 3 RIVALS BRAZIL ARE THE BOOKIES' **FAVOURITES** BUT THEY ARE STUNG BY AN EARLY COUNTER FROM CZECHOSLOVAKIA'S PETRAS. THE YOUNG **STRIKER** CROSSES HIMSELF IN CELEBRATION.

CUP **HOLDERS** ENGLAND ARE THOUGHT TO HAVE AN EVEN **BETTER** TEAM THAN '66. GEOFF HURST GETS THEIR SHOW ON THE **ROAD** AGAINST ROMANIA.

THE SOUTH AMERICANS THEN **SWAMP** THE CZECHS WITH SOME EXHILARATING **ATTACKING** FOOTBALL. THEIR FOUR GOALS INCLUDE A CRISP VOLLEY FROM PELE WHO IS APPEARING IN HIS **FOURTH** WORLD CUP.

'Fear no more the heat o' the sun' - **William Shakespeare**

BRAZIL'S CLASH WITH ENGLAND IS BILLED AS A DRESS **REHEARSAL** FOR THE FINAL. AFTER TEN MINUTES, THE FANS ARE TREATED TO A **BREATHTAKING** PIECE OF ACTION. CARLOS ALBERTO SENDS JAIRZINHO AWAY WITH AN **EXQUISITE** CURVING PASS.

PELE LEAPS LIKE A **SALMON** TO BULLET A HEADER TOWARDS THE CORNER OF THE NET. IT **LOOKS** A GOAL ALL THE WAY...

THE WINGER SPEEDS PAST FULL-BACK COOPER AND WHIPS OVER A HIGH **LOOPING** CROSS.

... UNTIL 'KEEPER GORDON BANKS **PLUNGES** FULL LENGTH TO SCOOP THE BALL UP AND **OVER** THE BAR. IT'S A QUITE MIRACULOUS SAVE.

THE **ENTHRALLING** CONTEST IS EVENTUALLY SETTLED IN THE SECOND HALF. PELE **TEES** THE BALL UP AND JAIRZINHO BLASTS HOME.

HAVING BEATEN ENGLAND, THERE LOOKS TO BE **NO STOPPING** BRAZIL. FREE-KICKS ARE THEIR SPECIALITY AND PELE PULLS ONE FROM THE **TOP DRAWER** IN THE 3-2 DEFEAT OF ROMANIA.

THAT **RESULT** LETS ENGLAND THROUGH TO MEET WEST GERMANY IN THE LAST EIGHT. BUT THERE IS A PRE-MATCH **BOMBSHELL** - STAR GOALIE BANKS GOES DOWN WITH FOOD POISONING.

HE IS SADLY **MISSED**. ENGLAND ARE CLINGING ONTO A 2-1 LEAD WHEN SEELER **SPECULATIVELY** FLIPS A BACK-HEADER TOWARDS GOAL. RESERVE 'KEEPER BONETTI IS IN NO-MAN'S LAND AS THE BALL **DROPS** OVER HIM.

'It was only when I saw the save later on TV that I realised it was a bit special' - Gordon Banks on his save from Pele

AS IN 1966, THE MATCH GOES TO **EXTRA-TIME** BUT ON THIS OCCASION IT'S THE GERMANS WHO HAVE THE LAST LAUGH. MULLER'S **MID-AIR** VOLLEY ENDS ENGLAND'S REIGN AS CHAMPIONS.

MEANWHILE, **BACK** IN GUADALAJARA, THE QUARTER AND SEMI-FINALS PROVE TO BE LITTLE MORE THAN A **SHOWPIECE** FOR BRAZIL'S SUMPTUOUS SKILLS. TOSTAO NETS **TWICE** IN THE WIN OVER PERU.

THERE IS MORE **INEPT** GOALKEEPING IN THE QUARTER-FINAL IN TOLUCA. MEXICAN 'KEEPER CALDERON, A PART-TIME MOVIE STAR, **FLUFFS** HIS LINES AS ITALY SLAM FOUR GOALS TO K.O. THE HOSTS.

WHILE, IN THE SEMI-FINAL, PELE PRODUCES AN **INGENIOUS** PIECE OF IMPROVISATION. HIS BRILLIANT DUMMY SELLS URUGUAY GOALIE MAZURKIEWICZ RIGHT **DOWN** THE RIVER.

THE OTHER SEMI-FINAL **UNFOLDS** INTO A CLIFF-HANGER. THE HEART-STOPPING **DRAMA** REALLY BEGINS IN INJURY TIME WHEN WEST GERMANY'S SCHNELLINGER EQUALISES **ITALY'S** EARLY GOAL.

WITH PLAYERS **RUNNING** ON EMPTY, STRIKES FROM BURGNICH AND RIVA RESTORE ITALY'S LEAD - UNTIL MULLER'S **TENTH** GOAL OF THE TOURNAMENT TIES IT YET AGAIN.

IN EXTRA-TIME, THE GERMANS ARE **HANDICAPPED** BY A SHOULDER INJURY TO BECKENBAUER BUT GOAL **MACHINE** MULLER STEALS IN TO SLIP THEM AHEAD.

THE **SEE-SAW** THEN TILTS FOR THE LAST TIME. IN THE 112TH MINUTE, RIVERA **SLOTS** THE *AZZURRI'S* FOURTH AND THE GERMANS HAVE **NOTHING** LEFT TO GIVE. ITALY ARE IN THE FINAL.

'The extra-time was like basketball' - Italian journalist after the semi-final

SUNDAY, JULY 21 AND **ALL ROADS** LEAD TO THE AZTECA STADIUM. CAN THE ITALIANS' RENOWNED DEFENCE CONTAIN BRAZIL'S **BUCCANEERING** FORWARDS?

ALMOST INEVITABLY, IT'S **PELE** WHO PROVIDES THE ANSWER. IN 17 MINUTES, THE MAESTRO JUMPS **SPECTACULARLY** TO HEAD HOME A TEASING RIVELINO CROSS.

BRAZIL ARE **CLEARLY** IN CHARGE BUT, CARELESSLY, THEY GIFT ITALY AN **EQUALISER** JUST BEFORE HALF-TIME.

IT'S MERELY A **STAY** OF EXECUTION. GERSON, THE SWEET-PASSING MIDFIELD GENERAL, THUMPS BRAZIL **IN FRONT** AGAIN AFTER 66 MINUTES.

WHEN PELE'S **ASSIST** ALLOWS JAIRZINHO TO RUN IN A THIRD, THE SAMBAS **STRIKE UP** IN EARNEST. JAIRZINHO HAS NOW SCORED IN **EVERY** ROUND.

THEN COMES THE **ICING** ON THE CAKE. PELE ROLLS THE BALL NONCHALANTLY INTO THE **PATH** OF CARLOS ALBERTO AND HIS SEARING DRIVE **FLIES** INTO THE CORNER OF THE NET - 4-1.

IT'S ALL OVER. PELE IS **CARRIED HIGH** BY JUBILANT FANS. IT'S THE PERFECT END TO A **GLORIOUS** WORLD CUP CAREER.

WITH PERHAPS THE FINEST **EXHIBITION** OF FLAIR FOOTBALL EVER SEEN, BRAZIL HAVE **WON** THE COVETED RIMET TROPHY FOR THE THIRD TIME. FITTINGLY, IT'S NOW **THEIRS** TO KEEP.

'Brazil '70 will always be remembered as the Team of the Century' - John Fashanu

Group 1

	P	W	D	L	F	A	Pts
USSR	3	2	1	0	6	1	5
Mexico	3	2	1	0	5	0	5
Belgium	3	1	0	2	4	5	2
El Salvador	3	0	0	3	0	9	0

Group 2

	P	W	D	L	F	A	Pts
Italy	3	1	2	0	1	0	4
Uruguay	3	1	1	1	2	1	3
Sweden	3	1	1	1	2	2	3
Israel	3	0	2	1	1	3	2

Group 3

	P	W	D	L	F	A	Pts
Brazil	3	3	0	0	8	3	6
England	3	2	0	1	2	1	4
Romania	3	1	0	2	4	5	2
Czechoslovakia	3	0	0	3	2	7	0

Group 4

	P	W	D	L	F	A	Pts
West Germany	3	3	0	0	10	4	6
Peru	3	2	0	1	7	5	4
Bulgaria	3	0	1	2	5	9	1
Morocco	3	0	1	2	2	6	1

Quarter-finals

Brazil	4	Peru	2
Uruguay	1	USSR	0 (*aet*)
West Germany	3	England	2 (*aet*)
Italy	4	Mexico	1

Semi-finals

Brazil	3	Uruguay	1
Italy	4	West Germany	3 (*aet*)

Third place play-off

West Germany	1	Uruguay	0

Final

Brazil	4	Italy	1

Brazil's superb victory in the Azteca Stadium created an unusual World Cup distinction for their manager **Mario Jorge Zagalo**.

Zagalo had been a member of the 1958 and 1962 Cup-winning teams and so, in 1970, he became the first man to win the trophy as both a player and a manager.

A calm and thorough 'technical director', he had actually arrived late on the scene, replacing Joao Saldanha as national boss only months before the Mexico finals.

And although he had some enormously talented players at his disposal, Zagalo must take credit for instilling an order which had previously been lacking in the Brazilian side.

His physical preparations too were impeccable – with the result that, despite the heat and altitude in Mexico, the Brazilians were consistently able to follow Zagalo's maxim: 'Attack at 85 miles an hour and defend at 105 miles an hour.'

The rest, of course, is history – after six straight victories, Brazil emerged as triumphant World Champions and any critics who had doubted Zagalo's appointment were left speechless.

But football is a fickle game and things did not run so smoothly for the Brazilian boss four years later in West Germany.

Deprived of several of the 1970 stars, Zagalo resorted to some uninspiring, defence-minded tactics and Brazil's fourth place was a flattering result. His dismissal followed soon after.

Zagalo later managed in the Middle East and steered the United Arab Emirates to the 1990 World Cup finals before being ungraciously sacked after a dispute with a UAE official.

- In 1970, Pele set a new record as the first man to appear for **three** World Cup winning sides, although injury had forced him to miss the climax of the 1962 tournament. In all, he scored 12 goals in his 14 World Cup finals appearances.

- Pele is also still the **youngest** player to score in the World Cup finals, but in 1982, Northern Ireland's Norman Whiteside, another 17-year-old, became the youngest-ever participant when he lined up against Yugoslavia.

- Brazil have competed in more tournaments than any other country – they're the only nation to have **taken part** in all 14 finals. Top European representatives are Germany and Italy with 12 finals appearances each.

- Another Brazilian record is that of most games **undefeated** (13 between 1958 and 1966). The longest sequence without a win in the finals belongs to hapless Bulgaria who have now played 16 matches without success.

- The top tournament for **goals** was undoubtedly the 1954 series in Switzerland. The net bulged140 times (an average of 5.38 goals per game) with Hungary scoring 27 of them – a record haul by any one team in the finals.

- The **highest score** in any World Cup match is New Zealand 13 Fiji 0 in the 1982 qualifying competition. Apparently, many of the happy-go-lucky Fijians were half-drunk on brandy after being dragged out of their hotel bar to play the game! New Zealand, meanwhile, clocked up a staggering 60,000-plus miles in qualifying for the finals.

- Mexican goalkeeper Antonio Carbajal appeared in a record **five tournaments** between 1950 and 1966. But Uwe Seeler of West Germany and Poland's Wladyslaw Zmuda have both played more matches – 21 each.

- Surprisingly, in **percentage terms**, the best finals record of any European nation belongs to Denmark. The dashing Danes won three of their four matches in *Mexico '86* – their first and only appearance to date – giving them a 75% overall success record. Italy come next with 68.52%.

- Diego Maradona was probably the sorest record-holder of the 1990 World Cup. He was the tournament's **'most-fouled player'** having been on the receiving end of no less than 53 unfair challenges.

- The **fewest** number of players used by a World Cup winning side is 12 – by Brazil in 1962. Indeed, had Pele not been hurt against Czechoslovakia, the same XI could well have appeared in all six matches. On the other extreme France gave all 22 of their squad an outing in 1978.

- The **oldest** man to win a World Cup medal is Dino Zoff, the 40-year-old goalkeeper who captained Italy in 1982. Another Italian 'keeper, Walter Zenga, holds the **'clean-sheet'** record, having played 517 minutes without conceding a goal during the 1990 finals.

WEST GERMANY

1974 WEST GERMANY

1974 AND THE WORLD CUP **BANDWAGON** ROLLS ON TO WEST GERMANY. A FLEET OF **LAVISHLY-DECORATED** BUSES FERRIES THE COMPETING TEAMS BETWEEN **NINE** CITIES.

FOR THE EVENTUAL WINNERS, THERE IS A **NEW PRIZE** WAITING. THE FIFA WORLD CUP REPLACES THE JULES RIMET TROPHY WON **OUTRIGHT** BY BRAZIL.

NOTABLE **ABSENTEES** ARE ENGLAND, OUSTED IN THE QUALIFYING COMPETITION BY POLAND. THE POLES ARE POTENTIAL **DARK** HORSES.

CHAMPIONS BRAZIL **BEGIN** THEIR DEFENCE AGAINST YUGOSLAVIA IN FRANKFURT. NOW MINUS PELE, THEY ARE A **SHADOW** OF THEIR FORMER SELVES AND ARE LUCKY TO **ESCAPE** WITH A 0-0 DRAW.

ONLY AN **AGONISING** MISS BY BREMNER ALLOWS BRAZIL TO AVOID DEFEAT BY SCOTLAND - BRITAIN'S **SOLE** REPRESENTATIVES. THE SCOTS BECOME THE FIRST COUNTRY TO BE ELIMINATED WITHOUT **LOSING** A MATCH.

DOWN IN MUNICH, IT TAKES A LATE **COMEBACK** TO SPARE ITALY'S BLUSHES. SANON HAD **EARLIER** FIRED THE UNKNOWNS OF HAITI INTO A SHOCK LEAD - MUCH TO THE **DELIGHT** TO THEIR SUBS BENCH.

MEANWHILE IN HAMBURG, **HISTORY** IS MADE AS WEST AND EAST GERMANY MEET FOR THE **FIRST** TIME.

SPARWASSER'S LATE STRIKE **SECURES** AN UNEXPECTED TRIUMPH FOR THE *DDR* BUT **BOTH** COUNTRIES PROGRESS TO THE SECOND PHASE GROUPS.

'There is neither East nor West when two strong men stand face to face' - Rudyard Kipling

THE TEAM REALLY **CATCHING** THE EYE IS HOLLAND, INSPIRED BY THE MERCURIAL JOHAN CRUYFF. THREE TIMES A EUROPEAN CUP **MEDALLIST** WITH AJAX AMSTERDAM, CRUYFF HAS SUCCEEDED PELE AS THE WORLD'S **TOP** PLAYER.

PLAYING A **FLUENT** TACTICAL STYLE KNOWN AS 'TOTAL FOOTBALL', THE DUTCH EFFORTLESSLY **SWEEP ASIDE** URUGUAY AND BULGARIA AS THEY ADVANCE.

IN THE SECOND ROUND, ARGENTINA ARE NEXT TO FEEL HOLLAND'S **AWESOME** GOAL POWER. CRUYFF WALTZES THROUGH TO NET THE FIRST IN A 4-0 **ROMP**.

AFTER EAST GERMANY ARE **COMFORTABLY** BEATEN 2-0, THE DUTCH ARE FIRMLY INSTALLED AS FAVOURITES. THEIR FANS ARE **SINGING** IN THE RAIN.

IRONICALLY, THE NEW **LEAGUE** FORMAT HAS SET UP A VIRTUAL SEMI-FINAL. - HOLLAND V BRAZIL - THE CHAMPIONS AGAINST THE **CHAMPIONS-ELECT**.

IT'S A TENSE, **NIGGLING** AFFAIR. BRAZIL SEEM INTENT ON DEFENDING THEIR CROWN AT **ALL COSTS**.

CLASS TELLS IN THE END. PLAYING A **CAPTAIN'S PART**, CRUYFF FEEDS NEESKENS TO END THE IMPASSE AND, 15 MINUTES LATER, HE **VOLLEYS** HOME A MAGNIFICENT SECOND GOAL.

BRAZIL'S **SHAMEFUL** FALL FROM GRACE IS COMPLETE AS PEREIRA IS **RED-CARDED**. THE FORMER KINGS OF FOOTBALL HAVE **SULLIED** THEIR REPUTATION BADLY. IT'S THE NEW BREED WHO GO **THROUGH** TO THE FINAL.

'The years of Total Football were among the finest played in the history of the game' - Brian Glanville

IN GROUP B, WEST GERMANY **STEP UP** A GEAR TO DEFEAT YUGOSLAVIA. THE **IRREPRESSIBLE** GERD MULLER SLIDES IN THE SECOND GOAL.

BUT, IN THE **ARCHETYPAL** 'GAME OF TWO HALVES', THE HOSTS' POWER PLAY TAKES THEM THROUGH **IN THE END**.

A **CRACKING** MATCH THEN FOLLOWS IN RAIN-DRENCHED DUSSELDORF. GERMANY ARE **ROCKED** BY EDSTROM'S SUPERB STRIKE FOR SWEDEN.

ONLY **POLAND** STAND IN THE GERMANS' WAY NOW. ON A **QUAGMIRE** PITCH, ONE **EXPLOSIVE** PIECE OF FINISHING FROM '*DER BOMBER*' MULLER DECIDES THE OUTCOME.

THE FINAL **SHOWDOWN** IS IN MUNICH'S FUTURISTIC OLYMPIC STADIUM. A RECORD 1,000 MILLION TV VIEWERS **TUNE IN** EXPECTANTLY.

HOLLAND BEGIN BY **CONFIDENTLY** KNOCKING THE BALL AROUND. THEN CRUYFF PICKS IT UP AND **BURSTS** SUDDENLY TOWARDS GOAL. HOENESS PANICS AND **LUNGES** RECKLESSLY.

THE **EXCITEMENT** HAS OBVIOUSLY AFFECTED THE GROUNDSTAFF. THEY HAVE **FORGOTTEN** TO PUT THE CORNER-FLAGS IN PLACE.

REFEREE **TAYLOR** BOLDLY POINTS TO THE SPOT - IT'S THE FIRST-EVER **PENALTY** AWARD IN A WORLD CUP FINAL. LESS THAN A **MINUTE** HAS BEEN PLAYED.

'Few toilets are used more often than those in the referee's room' - Jack Taylor

NEESKENS **BLASTS** HOME. FAVOURITES HOLLAND ARE IN FRONT.

BREITNER'S **ASSURED** SPOT-KICK MAKES IT 1-1. HAS THE TIDE NOW **TURNED**?

BUT GRADUALLY WEST GERMANY **CLAW** THEMSELVES BACK INTO THE MATCH. IN 25 MINUTES, THEIR **FAST-RAIDING** WINGER HOLZENBEIN TUMBLES AMID A FOREST OF ORANGE-CLAD LEGS - **ANOTHER** PENALTY!

MINUTES BEFORE HALF-TIME THE BALL COMES TO MULLER **INSIDE** THE DUTCH BOX. HE **SWIVELS**, SHOOTS AND THE BALL TRUNDLES PAST JONGBLOED TO COMPLETE A REMARKABLE **TURN-AROUND**.

AS THE TEAMS TROOP OFF, CRUYFF'S **FRUSTRATION** IS SHOWING. HE IS BOOKED BY TAYLOR AFTER SOME **EXCESSIVE** SPEECH-PLAY.

TIME **RUNS OUT** FOR THE DUTCH - LIKE HUNGARY IN '54, THEY HAVE FAILED TO TURN THEIR **SUPERIORITY** INTO GOLD.

PREDICTABLY, THE SECOND HALF SEES HOLLAND **PEPPER** THE GERMAN GOAL IN PURSUIT OF AN EQUALISER. BUT THE HOME DEFENCE STANDS **FIRM**.

NOT FOR THE FIRST TIME, GERMAN **RESILIENCE** HAS WON THE DAY. FRANZ BECKENBAUER, THEIR **STYLISH** CAPTAIN, PROUDLY DISPLAYS THE FRUIT OF THEIR LABOURS.

'All Gerd Muller ever does is hang about the penalty-area and score goals' - Olympic pentathlete Heidi Rosendahl

Group 1

	P	W	D	L	F	A	Pts
East Germany	3	2	1	0	4	1	5
West Germany	3	2	0	1	4	1	4
Chile	3	0	2	1	1	2	2
Australia	3	0	1	2	0	5	1

Group 2

	P	W	D	L	F	A	Pts
Yugoslavia	3	1	2	0	10	1	4
Brazil	3	1	2	0	3	0	4
Scotland	3	1	2	0	3	1	4
Zaire	3	0	0	3	0	14	0

Group 3

	P	W	D	L	F	A	Pts
Holland	3	2	1	0	6	1	5
Sweden	3	1	2	0	3	0	4
Bulgaria	3	0	2	1	2	5	2
Uruguay	3	0	1	2	1	6	1

Group 4

	P	W	D	L	F	A	Pts
Poland	3	3	0	0	12	3	6
Argentina	3	1	1	1	7	5	3
Italy	3	1	1	1	5	4	3
Haiti	3	0	0	3	2	14	0

Group A

	P	W	D	L	F	A	Pts
Holland	3	3	0	0	8	0	6
Brazil	3	2	0	1	3	3	4
East Germany	3	0	1	2	1	4	1
Argentina	3	0	1	2	2	7	1

Group B

	P	W	D	L	F	A	Pts
West Germany	3	3	0	0	7	2	6
Poland	3	2	0	1	3	2	4
Sweden	3	1	0	2	4	6	2
Yugoslavia	3	0	0	3	2	6	0

Third place play-off

Poland	1	Brazil	0

Final

West Germany	2	Holland	1

During his 14 years in charge of the West German national team, **Helmut Schoen** established himself as the most successful manager in modern World Cup history.

In the three tournaments between 1966 and 1974, the former international inside-forward led his country to first, second and third places.

Schoen certainly had the finest of apprenticeships in management, working as assistant to the legendary national coach Sepp Herberger in the years between 1956 and 1964.

He was therefore the natural choice as successor when the old master vacated the position in 1964.

But following Herberger was not an easy task and Schoen received his fair share of criticism during the early part of his tenure.

However he guided West Germany to the World Cup Final in 1966 and a highly-respectable third place in the 1970 tournament in Mexico.

His management philosophy of allowing players to express themselves with only the minimum of tactical restrictions was proving extremely effective.

In 1972, a star-studded West German line-up trounced the Soviet Union to take the European Championship title.

Although that side was perhaps past its peak by 1974, their experience, coupled with Schoen's ingenuity, helped them pull off that glorious World Cup triumph on home soil.

Unfortunately Schoen's swan-song, the 1978 tournament in Argentina, ended in severe anti-climax when the Germans exited the competition at the second phase.

Not surprisingly, he stuck to his pre-tournament decision to retire and thus pulled down the curtain on a highly-prosperous era for German football.

● Jack Taylor, a master butcher from Wolverhampton, was the third **Englishman** to referee a World Cup Final. Bill Ling officiated in the 1954 Final while George Reader was in charge of the Brazil-Uruguay 'final pool' decider in 1950. Reader, incidentally, was at that time considered **'too old'** to referee English League games.

● Referees were first mentioned in the **Laws of the Game** in 1874 and, four years later, came the first recorded use of a referee's whistle. When the English Football League began in 1888, a match official was paid a fee of 52.5 pence.

● The first referee to send a player off the field in a World Cup match was Chilean Alberto Warken in 1930. He gave **marching orders** to Peru captain Mario de Las Casas for violent play. Of the 13 other tournaments since, only the 1950 and 1970 finals were free of any orderings-off.

● The system of **yellow and red cards** was first introduced in 1970 after having been piloted in the 1968 Olympic Games football tournament. The first player to be red-carded in the finals was Chile's Carlos Caszely – for kicking West Germany's Berti Vogts in the 1974 match in Berlin.

● It's not often that football fans say a referee was faultless but they had to admit it during the 1954 World Cup. Scotland's **Charles Faultless** refereed two matches in the finals including the high-scoring Switzerland-Austria clash in Lausanne.

● Alexander Tukmanov, Vice President of the Soviet Football Federation, incurred the wrath of the men in black during the 1990 World Cup. Tukmanov offered to pay for **eye tests** for all the tournament's referees after Sweden's Erik Fredriksson had missed a clear handball by Diego Maradona in the Soviets' match against Argentina.

● **Politics** caused top Israeli whistler Abraham Klein to miss out on the 1978 Final between Argentina and Holland. The Argentinians complained about his selection because of Holland's political ties with Israel.

● Arthur Ellis, who had tried manfully to control the notorious 'Battle of Berne' in 1954, found some **easier arbitrating roles** after retiring from refereeing. He became a 'Pools Panel' forecaster and also officiated in 'It's a Knockout' – the British version of the pan-European television games show *Jeux Sans Frontieres.*

● Two cautionable offences should mean a sending-off, but in 1974 Australia's Raymond Richards was yellow-carded **twice** against Chile. He played on for five minutes before a linesman spilled the beans to the ref.

● On several occasions down the years football's governing bodies have toyed with the notion of deploying **two** referees. If the current wave of on-field discipline problems continues, it's an idea which could well be revived again.

ARGENTINA

1978 ARGENTINA

ARGENTINA'S MILITARY **DICTATORSHIP** MAKES FOR AN UNSTABLE BACKGROUND TO THE **1978** FINALS. FORTUNATELY THE COUNTRY'S LEFT-WING **GUERRILLAS** PROMISE NO VIOLENCE DURING THE COMPETITION.

FRANCE DON'T TAKE LONG TO FIND THE WAY TO GOAL. LACOMBE **PLANTS** A HEADER IN THE ITALIAN NET AFTER JUST 31 **SECONDS**. ITALY RECOVER TO WIN 2-1.

FOR THE **FOURTH** CONSECUTIVE TOURNAMENT, THE OPENING MATCH FINISHES **0-0**. WEST GERMANY AND POLAND BORE MILLIONS WITH A **DRAB** GAME.

IN BUENOS AIRES, A **BLINDING** TICKER-TAPE STORM GREETS THE HOSTS ARGENTINA. WILL MANAGER MENOTTI'S EMPHASIS ON **CULTURED** FOOTBALL PAY DIVIDENDS?

ARGENTINA BEGIN WITH A 2-1 **WIN** OVER HUNGARY, BUT IN THEIR NEXT MATCH, THEY NEED A **SPECIAL** STRIKE FROM LUQUE TO OVERCOME THE UNLUCKY FRENCH.

BRAZIL **PLOD** THROUGH THE FIRST-ROUND WITH JUST ONE VICTORY. THEY WOULD'VE BEATEN SWEDEN HAD **REFEREE** THOMAS NOT BLOWN FOR FULL-TIME SECONDS **BEFORE** ZICO HEADED IN A CORNER.

WITH **BOTH** COUNTRIES ASSURED OF QUALIFICATION, ONLY LATIN **PRIDE** IS AT STAKE IN THE ARGENTINA-ITALY CLASH. BETTEGA'S **FINE** GOAL MEANS THE *AZZURRI* WILL STAY ON IN THE CAPITAL.

IN CORDOBA, SCOTLAND, FULL OF PRE-TOURNAMENT **PROMISE**, PERFORM MISERABLY AGAINST PERU AND IRAN. MANAGER MACLEOD'S NORMAL EXUBERANCE TURNS TO **DESPAIR**.

'The execution squad is probably waiting for me back home' - Ally MacLeod

THERE IS **FURTHER** EMBARRASS-MENT FOR THE SCOTS WHEN WINGER WILLIE JOHNSTON FAILS A DRUGS TEST AND **CATCHES** AN EARLY PLANE HOME.

BUT SCOTLAND **ALMOST** PULL OFF A REMARKABLE TRIUMPH OVER ADVERSITY. GEMMILL'S **CLASSIC** SOLO GOAL GIVES THEM VICTORY OVER HOLLAND WHO GO THROUGH ONLY ON **GOAL DIFFERENCE**.

HOLLAND AT THIS STAGE ARE SHORT ON **CONFIDENCE** AND MISSING JOHAN CRUYFF. EVEN A SPECIALLY-COMPOSED SONG FAILED TO MAKE HIM **RECONSIDER** HIS DECISION NOT TO TRAVEL.

IN THE SECOND PHASE THOUGH, THE DUTCH **BEGIN** TO FIND SOME FORM. WILLY VAN DE KERKHOF ROUNDS OFF A 5-1 **DESTRUCTION** OF AUSTRIA.

HOLLAND THEN MEET WEST GERMANY IN AN **ACTION-PACKED** RE-RUN OF THE 1974 FINAL. THE GERMANS LOOK TO BE SNEAKING A CRUCIAL **VICTORY** UNTIL RENE VAN DE KERKHOF, WILLY'S TWIN BROTHER, **DANCES** THROUGH TO EQUALISE.

OVERALL, THE HOLDERS HAVE BEEN **DISAPPOINTING**. THEIR SLIM HOPES OF REACHING THE FINAL ARE **DASHED** BY TWO GOALS FROM AUSTRIA'S HANS KRANKL.

THE HOLLAND-ITALY MATCH WILL **DECIDE** THE ALL-EUROPEAN SEMI-FINAL GROUP. DUTCHMAN ERNIE BRANDTS PRODUCES A WORLD CUP **NOVELTY** BY SCORING FOR BOTH TEAMS.

WITH 14 MINUTES LEFT ARIE HAAN, AN **ACCOMPLISHED** LONG-RANGE MARKSMAN, UNLEASHES A **HOWITZER** TO CLINCH HOLLAND'S PLACE IN THE FINAL. CAN THEY GO **ONE BETTER** THAN LAST TIME?

'I told you all along this team was not as good as the 1974 side' - Helmut Schoen

ARGENTINA FACE POLAND IN THE FIRST **GROUP B** FIXTURE. WITH LUQUE INJURED, MUCH IS EXPECTED OF **FELLOW** STRIKER MARIO **KEMPES** ON HIS OLD STOMPING GROUND AT ROSARIO.

BRAZIL ARE THE **OBVIOUS** CHALLENGERS TO ARGENTINA. BUT, OVERCOME BY FEAR OF LOSING, THE TEAMS PLAY OUT A **SCRAPPY** AND OFTEN-BRUTAL 0-0 DRAW.

KEMPES **DELIVERS** THE GOODS. HE SEES OFF THE POLES WITH TWO **EMPHATIC** FINISHES.

NOW GOAL DIFFERENCE WILL **DETERMINE** THE FINALISTS. BRAZIL, KICKING OFF EARLY, BEAT POLAND 3-1. ARGENTINA KNOW THEIR TARGET - THEY MUST **SCORE FOUR** TIMES AGAINST PERU.

STANDING IN THEIR WAY IS **ECCENTRIC** PERU 'KEEPER QUIROGA. THE MADCAP GOALIE HAD BEEN **BOOKED** AGAINST POLAND FOR FOULING IN THE POLISH HALF OF THE PITCH.

THE **ATMOSPHERE** IN ROSARIO IS ELECTRIC. PERU WORRY THE HOSTS EARLY ON BUT IN THE 21ST MINUTE, KEMPES **BUSTLES** THROUGH TO SHOOT ARGENTINA AHEAD.

THEREAFTER, IT'S STRICTLY **ONE-WAY** TRAFFIC. PERU COLLAPSE AND ARGENTINA RAM IN **FIVE MORE** GOALS. BRAZIL, UNDERSTANDABLY INCENSED, **ALLEGE** THAT THE PERUVIANS HAVE BEEN 'BOUGHT'.

THE **FANATICAL** ARGENTINIAN PUBLIC COULDN'T CARE LESS. THEIR **HEROES** ARE IN THE FINAL AND BUENOS AIRES IS BUZZING.

'We'll be on the pitch to beat Argentina, not to give the match away to them' - Peru coach Marcos Calderon

BEFORE THE KICK-OFF, ARGENTINA INDULGE IN SOME **PSYCHOLOGICAL** WARFARE. THEY KEEP HOLLAND WAITING AND THEN **OBJECT** TO A **SMALL** PLASTER ON THE HAND OF RENE VAN DE KERKHOF.

THE DUTCH ARE **NOT** AMUSED AND THERE ARE SOME NASTY EARLY **EXCHANGES**.

IN THE 38TH MINUTE, **ACE-IN-THE-PACK** KEMPES MAKES THE BREAKTHROUGH FOR ARGENTINA. HE **DODGES** KROL'S TACKLE AND **ROLLS** THE BALL UNDER JONGBLOED.

HOLLAND HAVE THE **BETTER** OF THE SECOND HALF. A LONG-THREATENED EQUALISER FINALLY **ARRIVES** FROM THE HEAD OF TOWERING SUBSTITUTE NANNINGA.

IN THE DYING SECONDS, RESENBRINK COMES **TANTALIS-INGLY** CLOSE TO AN HISTORIC WINNER WHEN HE HITS THE POST FROM JUST **FIVE YARDS**. THE MATCH GOES INTO EXTRA-TIME.

HOLLAND'S SECOND-HALF **EXERTIONS** HAVE LEFT THEM DRAINED. AFTER FOURTEEN MINUTES, KEMPES **WRIGGLES** PAST THREE DUTCHMEN TO FORCE ARGENTINA **BACK** INTO THE LEAD.

THE **POWERHOUSE** STRIKER IS RAMPANT NOW. SIX MINUTES FROM THE END HE CLEAVES ANOTHER **HOLE** IN THE DUTCH DEFENCE AND BERTONI DELIVERS THE *COUP DE GRACE*.

HOLLAND ARE THE **NEARLY-MEN** AGAIN. THE ARGENTINIANS MEANWHILE, CAN **FORGET** ALL THEIR POLITICAL AND ECONOMIC PROBLEMS AND **REJOICE** IN WORLD CUP VICTORY AT LONG LAST.

'But for Kempes, we would be champions now' - Holland's Johan Neeskens

Group 1

	P	W	D	L	F	A	Pts
Italy	3	3	0	0	6	2	6
Argentina	3	2	0	1	4	3	4
France	3	1	0	2	5	5	2
Hungary	3	0	0	3	3	8	0

Group 2

	P	W	D	L	F	A	Pts
Poland	3	2	1	0	4	1	5
West Germany	3	1	2	0	6	0	4
Tunisia	3	1	1	1	3	2	3
Mexico	3	0	0	3	2	12	0

Group 3

	P	W	D	L	F	A	Pts
Austria	3	2	0	1	3	2	4
Brazil	3	1	2	0	2	1	4
Spain	3	1	1	1	2	2	3
Sweden	3	0	1	2	1	3	1

Group 4

	P	W	D	L	F	A	Pts
Peru	3	2	1	0	7	2	5
Holland	3	1	1	1	5	3	3
Scotland	3	1	1	1	5	6	3
Iran	3	0	1	2	2	8	1

Group A

	P	W	D	L	F	A	Pts
Holland	3	2	1	0	9	4	5
Italy	3	1	1	1	2	2	3
West Germany	3	0	2	1	4	5	2
Austria	3	1	0	2	4	8	2

Group B

	P	W	D	L	F	A	Pts
Argentina	3	2	1	0	8	0	5
Brazil	3	2	1	0	6	1	5
Poland	3	1	0	2	2	5	2
Peru	3	0	0	3	0	10	0

Third place play-off

Brazil	2	Italy	1

Final

Argentina	3	Holland	1 (aef)

Prior to the 1978 World Cup, Argentina had one of the worst reputations in international football.

A long history of disputes with FIFA and some unsavoury on-field tactics had firmly established the Argentinians as the 'bad boys' of world soccer.

In a few short weeks of 1978, much of that was changed – thanks largely to the efforts of one individual – their charismatic, chain-smoking manager **Cesar Luis Menotti**.

Very much 'his own man', Menotti had fought many battles with the authorities in assembling his squad for the tournament.

He had also caused something of a sensation throughout South America by not calling on his exiles, Kempes excepted, and by ignoring players from the Argentinian Champions – the popular Boca Juniors.

In addition, Menotti had to make the brave decision of leaving out the brilliant 17-year-old Diego Maradona because he was too young.

Above all though, it was Menotti's unflinching belief in positive football and in the inherent skill of his Argentinian players that earned him most respect.

Argentina won the 1978 World Cup largely because they were the side which most consistently adhered to the philosophy of attacking play.

Menotti also led his country in 1982, but when the ageing side failed to retain the trophy, he made way for Carlos Bilardo to take the reins.

After managing leading clubs in both South America and Spain, Menotti returned to the international scene in 1991 as national coach of Mexico.

He successfully launched their '94 World Cup qualifying campaign before resigning over differences with their FA officials.

● The van de Kerkhofs who played for Holland against Argentina in 1978 were the fourth **set of brothers** to play together in a World Cup Final. Coincidentally, in the second phase, the twins had each scored in the 83rd minute of matches against Austria and West Germany respectively. Willy is the older of the two – by 50 minutes!

● The **first** brothers to win a World Cup medal were West Germany's Fritz and Ottmar Walter in 1954. Fritz, a wartime paratrooper, captained the side which shocked Hungary by winning 3-2 in Berne. 24 years earlier, Argentina's losing side in the 1930 Final had included the Evaristo brothers, Juan and Mario.

● Bobby and Jack Charlton, England's heroes of 1966, had an impressive footballing **heritage**. Four of their uncles played professional soccer and their mother's cousin was Jackie Milburn – the famous 1950s centre-forward of Newcastle United. Jack Charlton has managed the Republic of Ireland team since 1986.

● In 1930, Mexican defenders Manuel and Felipe Rosas **made history** as the first brothers to play together in the World Cup when they teamed-up against France. Later in the tournament, Manuel converted the World Cup's first-ever penalty in Mexico's 6-3 defeat by Argentina.

● Brazil is the only nation to have been **managed** by two brothers in the World Cup finals. Zeze Moreira was in charge of their team in 1954 while brother Aimore bossed the victorious 1962 side. Moving up to date, current Brazilian hero Rai is the younger brother of 1982 star Socrates.

● Andre Abegglen, who played for Switzerland in the 1934 and 1938 World Cups, was one of **three** famous footballing brothers. Another of them, Max 'Xam' Abegglen was a founding member of Xamax Neuchatel and it's to him that the Swiss club owes its unusual, palindromic name.

● Cameroon's Biyick brothers completed a unique **fraternal double** in the opening match of the 1990 tournament. In the 65th minute, Francois Omam Biyick headed the Africans' winner against Argentina – five minutes after brother Andre Kana had been ordered off.

● The 1990 Holland v Egypt match saw two sets of brothers in **opposition**. Egypt fielded Hossam and Ibrahim Hassan while the Dutch included Erwin and Ronald Koeman in their line-up.

● The last brothers to appear together in a Final were the Forsters, Bernd and Karlheinz, who were part of West Germany's line-up in 1982. Eighteen months earlier, they had **exploited** their similarity in a mischievous way during a UEFA Cup match. Bernd pretended to be Karlheinz after the latter had committed a second cautionable offence and thus faced a sending-off. Not surprisingly, they were both suspended by UEFA!

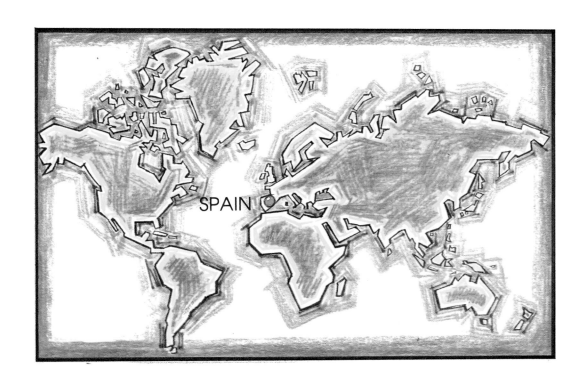

SPAIN

1982 SPAIN

REACTING TO **PRESSURE** FROM THIRD WORLD MEMBERS, FIFA EXPAND THE 1982 FINALS TO TAKE IN **24 TEAMS**. THE DRAW HOWEVER IS A FARCE. SCOTLAND ARE **PULLED OUT** TO PLAY ARGENTINA AND THEN RE-LOCATED INTO **BRAZIL'S** GROUP.

IT'S **BELGIUM** WHO EVENTUALLY FACE THE CUP HOLDERS IN THE **OPENING** GAME IN BARCELONA. THE MATCH BUCKS THE TREND FOR 0-0 DRAWS WITH VANDENBERGH'S **SOLITARY** GOAL ENOUGH TO BEAT THE ARGENTINIANS.

BOTH THESE TEAMS **QUALIFY** FROM THEIR GROUP. HUNGARY GO OUT DESPITE THEIR 10-1 **MAULING** OF EL SALVADOR - A NEW RECORD SCORE IN THE FINALS.

OF THE **FIRST-TIME** PARTICIPANTS, ALGERIA MAKE THE BIGGEST **IMPACT**. THEY HUMBLE 1974 WINNERS WEST GERMANY.

FRUSTRATINGLY FOR THE ALGERIANS, THEY ARE ELIMINATED BY WHAT LOOKS LIKE AN UNSPORTING PIECE OF **COLLUSION**. THE GERMANS AND AUSTRIA TAMELY PLAY OUT THEIR MATCH AFTER A **MUTUALLY-SUITABLE** SCORELINE IS ESTABLISHED.

OTHER **NEW BOYS** CAMEROON BRIGHTEN UP PROCEEDINGS WITH SOME IMPRESSIVE FOOTBALL AND LIVELY **ANTICS**.

ULTIMATELY, THE **UNDEFEATED** AFRICANS ARE ONLY REMOVED BECAUSE ITALY HAVE **SCORED** MORE GOALS. WITH THREE STRAIGHT DRAWS, THE *AZZURRI* HAVE MADE AN **INAUSPICIOUS** START TO THE CAMPAIGN.

UP IN BILBAO, ENGLAND TAKE **JUST** 27 SECONDS TO NOTCH THEIR FIRST FINALS GOAL FOR **12 YEARS**. BRYAN ROBSON CATCHES FRANCE ON THE **HOP**.

'There is no FIFA rule saying teams cannot play as they please' - *Hermann Neuberger, German FA president*

THE FRENCH HAVE **PROBLEMS** OF A DIFFERENT KIND IN THEIR NEXT MATCH. KUWAIT'S **PRINCE** FAHID MANAGES TO PERSUADE THE REFEREE TO **DISALLOW** A GOAL AGAINST HIS SIDE.

THE SPANISH **FANS** ARE ENJOYING THE FOOTBALL FIESTA BUT ARE **DISAPPOINTED** IN THE **FORM** OF THEIR OWN TEAM. IN A MEMORABLE MATCH, **UNFANCIED** NORTHERN IRELAND BEAT THEM 1-0.

AS THE FIRST ROUND **ENDS,** DEFINITE **FAVOURITES** HAVE EMERGED. BRAZIL, EXHIBITING THEIR SAMBA SOCCER OF **OLD**, PROVE MUCH TOO GOOD FOR THE SOVIET UNION AND **GALLANT** SCOTLAND.

IN THE **THREE-TEAM** SECOND ROUND GROUP, BRAZIL FINALLY KNOCK OFF ARGENTINA'S **TOPPLING** CROWN. JUNIOR ACCLAIMS HIS CLASSIC GOAL WITH A **DANCE** OF DELIGHT.

ARGENTINIAN **STARLET** MARADONA VENTS HIS FRUSTRATION WITH A **SPITEFUL** FOUL AND DEPARTS THE TOURNAMENT IN **DISGRACE.** HIS DAY WILL COME.

BRAZIL NOW NEED ONLY A DRAW TO REACH THE **RE-INTRODUCED** SEMI-FINALS. BLOCKING THEIR WAY - THE ITALIANS WHOSE **IRON-MAN** DEFENDER GENTILE HAS JUST GIVEN MARADONA A **HARSH** INTRODUCTION TO WORLD CUP FOOTBALL.

DISPLAYING A **REFRESHINGLY** ATTACK-MINDED ATTITUDE, ITALY FIND THEMSELVES 2-1 **AHEAD** AT HALF-TIME. PAOLO ROSSI TWICE MAKES **CAPITAL** OUT OF BRAZIL'S DEFENSIVE INDISCRETIONS.

BUT IN 68 MINUTES, FALCAO **CRACKS** HOME A ROCKET TO TIE THE EPIC GAME AT 2-2. BRAZILIAN **DRUMS** - AND HEARTS - BEAT AGAIN. CAN THEIR TEAM NOW HOLD OUT FOR THE **POINT** THEY NEED?

'Somebody's going to have to come up with something sensational for us' - Northern Ireland's Gerry Armstrong after the draw.

CRUCIALLY, THE SOUTH AMERICANS' REARGUARD FAILS THEM ONCE **MORE**. THEY **STRUGGLE** TO CLEAR A CORNER AND ROSSI POUNCES TO TURN THE BALL PAST PERES. THE CARNIVAL IS **OVER**.

ROSSI'S **GLORIOUS** HAT-TRICK HAS CAPPED A SENSATIONAL RETURN TO INTERNATIONAL SOCCER. HE **MISSED** TWO SEASONS AFTER BEING SUSPENDED ON **BRIBERY** CHARGES.

MEANWHILE IN MADRID, ENGLAND **MUST** BEAT SPAIN TO STAY **ALIVE** IN THE TOURNAMENT. KEEGAN'S CLUMSY MISS **ALLOWS** WEST GERMANY TO QUALIFY FROM THAT GROUP.

THE SEVILLE SEMI-FINAL **PITCHES** GERMAN GRIT AGAINST FRENCH WIT. IN 18 MINUTES, **LITTBARSKI** THREADS HOME THE OPENER.

WITH THE SCORES **LEVEL** AT 1-1, GERMAN 'KEEPER SCHUMACHER COMMITS AN **ATROCIOUS** FOUL ON FRANCE'S BATTISTON. INCREDIBLY, THE REFEREE TAKES **NO** ACTION.

THE **HIGH-OCTANE** ACTION ROLLS ON INTO EXTRA-TIME. FRANCE STRIKE **TWICE** THROUGH TIGANA AND GIRESSE AND, NATURALLY, THEY **SENSE** VICTORY.

BUT THE GERMANS **DEFY** THE ODDS YET AGAIN. SUBSTITUTE RUMMENIGGE PULLS ONE BACK AND FISCHER'S **ACROBATIC** EFFORT MAKES IT 3-3.

FOR THE FIRST TIME EVER, A PENALTY **SHOOT-OUT** WILL DECIDE THE FINALISTS. SOCCER'S VERSION OF **RUSSIAN ROULETTE** BRINGS AGONY FOR THE OFF-TARGET BOSSIS AND **ECSTASY** FOR HRUBESCH WHO CONVERTS GERMANY'S **WINNING** KICK.

'God's judgement willed that luck fell on the German side in that game' - Chancellor Helmut Schmidt

THE OTHER SEMI IS A **SEDATE** AFFAIR BY COMPARISON. PRODIGAL SON ROSSI **CONTINUES** TO BE ITALY'S DECISIVE HIT-MAN AGAINST POLAND.

THE **CIRCUMSTANCES** OF WEST GERMANY'S ADVANCE TO THE FINAL HAS MADE THEM UNPOPULAR. THE **VASTLY-IMPROVED** ITALIANS WILL ENJOY THE MAJORITY OF THE **BACKING** IN THE MAGNIFICENT BERNABEU STADIUM.

AFTER 25 **HIGHLY**-FORGETTABLE MINUTES, THE *AZZURRI* PASS UP A **GILT-EDGED** CHANCE TO TAKE THE LEAD WHEN CABRINI **SLICES** HIS PENALTY WIDE. IS FORTUNE STILL FAVOURING THE GERMANS?

WITH ALMOST AN **HOUR** GONE, IT LOOKS DIFFICULT TO PICK A WINNER. THEN **ENTER** *SIGNOR* ROSSI. FROM A GENTILE CROSS, HE DIVES **HEADLONG** TO FORCE THE BALL OVER THE LINE. 1-0 TO ITALY.

THE GERMANS **RESPOND** BUT, IN THE 68TH MINUTE, MARCO TARDELLI MAKES A **TELLING** CONTRIBUTION. HE FINDS ROOM ON THE **EDGE** OF THE BOX AND HIS SCREAMING LEFT-FOOT DRIVE **WHIZZES** PAST SCHUMACHER.

THE **HARD-WORKING** MIDFIELDER CAN HARDLY BELIEVE IT. ITALY ARE SURELY ON THEIR WAY TO A **THIRD** WORLD CUP VICTORY.

NINE MINUTES FROM **TIME** ALTOBELLI **ROUNDS OFF** THE NIGHT BY HAMMERING IN A THIRD GOAL. IT'S ALL OVER **BAR** THE SHOUTING.

BREITNER'S **LATE** COUNTER IS INCONSEQUENTIAL. **40-YEAR OLD** GOALKEEPER-CAPTAIN DINO ZOFF HOISTS THE CUP - A SIGHT WHICH HAD LOOKED DECIDEDLY **UNLIKELY** THREE WEEKS EARLIER.

'A World Cup without a happy-end!' - Nuremberg-based Fussball Magazin

Group 1

	P	W	D	L	F	A	Pts
Poland	3	1	2	0	5	1	4
Italy	3	0	3	0	2	2	3
Cameroon	3	0	3	0	1	1	3
Peru	3	0	2	1	2	6	2

Group 2

	P	W	D	L	F	A	Pts
West Germany	3	2	0	1	6	3	4
Austria	3	2	0	1	3	1	4
Algeria	3	2	0	1	5	5	4
Chile	3	0	0	3	3	8	0

Group 3

	P	W	D	L	F	A	Pts
Belgium	3	2	1	0	3	1	5
Argentina	3	2	0	1	6	2	4
Hungary	3	1	1	1	12	6	3
El Salvador	3	0	0	3	1	13	0

Group 4

	P	W	D	L	F	A	Pts
England	3	3	0	0	6	1	6
France	3	1	1	1	6	5	3
Czechoslovakia	3	0	2	1	2	4	2
Kuwait	3	0	1	2	2	6	1

Group 5

	P	W	D	L	F	A	Pts
Northern Ireland	3	1	2	0	2	1	4
Spain	3	1	1	1	3	3	3
Yugoslavia	3	1	1	1	2	2	3
Honduras	3	0	2	1	2	3	2

Group 6

	P	W	D	L	F	A	Pts
Brazil	3	3	0	0	10	2	6
USSR	3	1	1	1	6	4	3
Scotland	3	1	1	1	8	8	3
New Zealand	3	0	0	3	2	12	0

Group A

	P	W	D	L	F	A	Pts
Poland	2	1	1	0	3	0	3
USSR	2	1	1	0	1	0	3
Belgium	2	0	0	2	0	4	0

Group B

	P	W	D	L	F	A	Pts
West Germany	2	1	1	0	2	1	3
England	2	0	2	0	0	0	2
Spain	2	0	1	1	1	2	1

Group C

	P	W	D	L	F	A	Pts
Italy	2	2	0	0	5	3	4
Brazil	2	1	0	1	5	4	2
Argentina	2	0	0	2	2	5	0

Group D

	P	W	D	L	F	A	Pts
France	2	2	0	0	5	1	4
Austria	2	0	1	1	2	3	1
Northern Ireland	2	0	1	1	3	6	1

Semi-finals

Italy	2	Poland	0
West Germany	3	France	3

(*aet – West Germany won on penalties*)

Third place play-off

Poland	3	France	2

Final

Italy	3	West Germany	1

Italy's fine victory in Madrid proved especially sweet for their manager **Enzo Bearzot**.

After indifferent performances in the first-round, discernible tension had built up between Bearzot and the highly-critical Italian media and the *Azzurri's* eventual triumph brought relief as much as joy for the former Torino star.

Managing the Italian side is one of the hardest jobs in world football – mainly due to the mammoth expectations of the nation's soccer-mad public – but Bearzot acquitted himself well during his time with the *FIGC*.

After taking charge in 1977, Bearzot led Italy to an impressive fourth place in the 1978 World Cup in Argentina where they were the only country to inflict a defeat on the hosts during the tournament.

Their success in Spain, four years later, was something of a personal triumph for the gaunt and careworn-looking Bearzot.

He had contrived to free the talented national squad players from the defensive mentality inherent in Italian domestic football and this fresh, aggressive attitude delivered the most tangible of rewards.

A respected man-manager, Bearzot must also be credited with keeping faith with striker Paolo Rossi who had spent two years in the soccer wilderness through suspension.

Bearzot directed Italy's defence of their title four years later in Mexico but, ironically, despite a sound start in that tournament, his side flopped badly in the second round.

Azeglio Vicini, for years Bearzot's senior aide, succeeded him as national manager after the '86 World Cup.

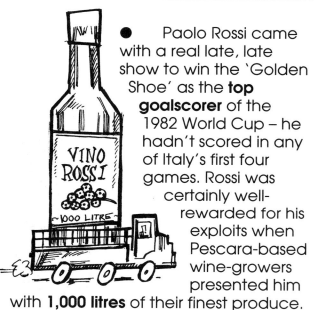

● Paolo Rossi came with a real late, late show to win the 'Golden Shoe' as the **top goalscorer** of the 1982 World Cup – he hadn't scored in any of Italy's first four games. Rossi was certainly well-rewarded for his exploits when Pescara-based wine-growers presented him with **1,000 litres** of their finest produce.

● West Germany's Gerd Muller holds the **aggregate** record for World Cup finals goals with 14 (10 in 1970 plus 4 in 1974). After finishing his playing career in the North American Soccer League, 'Der Bomber' took to catering and became a restaurant manager in Fort Lauderdale, Florida.

● Just Fontaine's **individual** record of 13 goals in one tournament is unlikely ever to be beaten. A native of Marrakesh, Morocco, he scored in every one of France's six matches during the 1958 World Cup. Amazingly, Fontaine had travelled to Sweden fully expecting to be a reserve and only secured his place in the side after an injury to fellow striker Rene Biliard.

● The top scorer in the 1966 World Cup also hailed from **Africa.** Portugal's Eusebio Ferreira da Silva was born in their old colony of Mozambique and was snapped up by Lisbon giants Benfica as a 19-year-old. In 1968 Eusebio became the first winner of the 'Golden Boot' award for Europe's leading club goalscorer.

● It is generally thought that, in 1970, Jairzinho of Brazil became the first player to score in **every round** including the Final. However Uruguay's right-winger Alcide Ghiggia netted in all his country's matches in 1950, including the final pool decider against Brazil.

● Guillermo Stabile of Argentina is credited with the first-ever World Cup **hat-trick**, scored against Mexico in 1930. Hungary's Laszlo Kiss can claim the fastest – he took only nine minutes to bag three against El Salvador in 1982. The Hungarian's feat is all the more remarkable since he was a substitute in the match.

● In the 1978 World Cup, the tournament's leading marksman, Mario Kempes, showed he was capable of **saving** goals as well as scoring them. In Argentina's match with Poland, Kempes made a superb diving 'save' to deny the Poles a goal. Their captain Deyna missed the resultant penalty.

● Italy's 'Toto' Schillaci can **thank** team-mate Roberto Baggio for helping him top the goal charts in Italia '90. When the *Azzurri* were awarded a penalty in the third place match against England, regular spot-kick expert Baggio said to Schillaci: 'Toto, you take it. I want you to be the top scorer.'

● Because of less-reliable timing in the earlier tournaments, there is some dispute about the **quickest** goal ever scored in the finals. However, Bryan Robson's goal in 27 seconds, for England against France in 1982, is undoubtedly the fastest strike in modern World Cup history. The Manchester United midfielder earned himself an imposing gold watch for his extra-early effort.

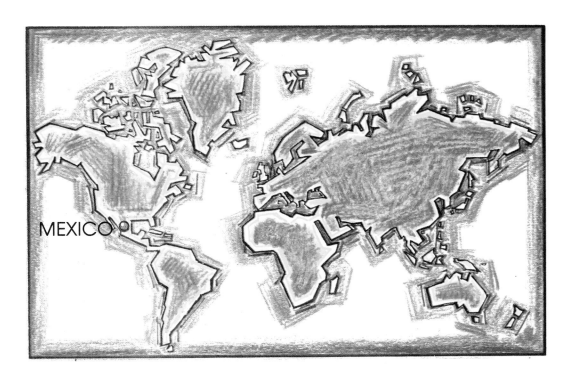

MEXICO

1986 MEXICO

WHEN **ORIGINAL** HOSTS COLOMBIA CALL OFF, MEXICO BECOMES THE FIRST COUNTRY TO STAGE THE FINALS **TWICE**. A NEW CROWD PHENOMENON APPEARS - **THE WAVE**.

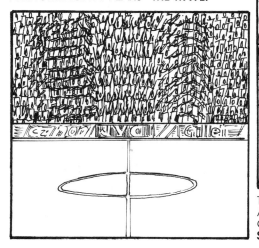

THE **FERVENT** MEXICAN FANS ARE, AS EVER, ANTICIPATING GREAT THINGS FROM THEIR OWN SIDE. HOPES ARE **PINNED** ON **SOMERSAULTING** STRIKER HUGO SANCHEZ.

MUCH IS ALSO **EXPECTED** FROM DIEGO MARADONA. THE ARGENTINIAN CAPTAIN HAS **MATURED** SINCE '82 AND IS NOW DEMONSTRATING FOOTBALL **ARTISTRY** REMINISCENT OF PELE IN HIS HEYDAY.

IN A **BETTER-THAN-USUAL** CURTAIN-RAISER, ITALY'S ALTOBELLI PICKS UP FROM WHERE HE **LEFT OFF** IN MADRID. BULGARIA LATER DRAW LEVEL.

ENGLAND MAKE A **STUTTERING** START IN A **DREARY** GROUP. THEY MUDDLE THROUGH BUT LOSE **SKIPPER** ROBSON AND VICE-CAPTAIN WILKINS THROUGH **INJURY** AND SUSPENSION.

THE **HIGH POINT** OF THE FIRST ROUND IS THE SCINTILLATING PERFORMANCE OF **FIRST-TIMERS** DENMARK. LAUDRUP SCORES A VIRTUOSO FOURTH GOAL IN THE HIGHLY-POPULAR **DISMANTLING** OF BAD-BOYS URUGUAY.

THE DANES ARE IN **DEVASTATING** FORM, AND, AFTER BEATING WEST GERMANY, ARE **WIDELY-TIPPED** AS POTENTIAL WINNERS. 'WE'RE RED, WE'RE WHITE, WE'RE **DYNAMITE**!' **CHANT** THEIR COLOURFUL FANS - THE ROLIGANS.

BUT **SADLY** FOR FOOTBALL-LOVERS, THE WHEELS SOON **COME OFF** THE DANISH BANDWAGON. AFTER THEY TAKE THE LEAD AGAINST SPAIN, OLSEN'S **SLACK** PASS **PRESENTS** AN EQUALISER TO BUTRAGUENO.

'This is what the fans want to see - not actors, cheats and massed defences' - Denmark's Preben Elkjaer

AS DENMARK **CHASE** THE GAME, 'THE VULTURE' BUTRAGUENO **SWOOPS** TO SCORE THREE MORE TIMES. IT'S A RECORD-EQUALLING **PERSONAL** HAUL AND A SPLENDID 5-1 VICTORY FOR SPAIN IN THE NEW **ALL-KNOCK-OUT** SECOND PHASE.

IN **ANOTHER** EXCELLENT MATCH, USSR AND BELGIUM LAY ON A **GRIPPING** END-TO-END SPECTACLE FOR THE LEON PUBLIC. **BELANOV** BLASTS A HAT-TRICK FOR THE SOVIETS.

BUT THE **COUNTER-PUNCHING** BELGIANS HAVE THEIR ANSWERS READY. DEMOL'S **WELL-DIRECTED** HEADER PAVES THE WAY FOR A 4-3 EXTRA-TIME WIN.

BACK IN MEXICO CITY, **HOLDERS** ITALY BOW OUT QUIETLY. THEY YIELD TO THE SUPERIOR **FINESSE** OF THE FRENCH AND THEIR HIGHLY-CREATIVE NO.10, MICHEL **PLATINI**.

FRANCE'S QUARTER-FINAL WITH BRAZIL IS A REAL **CORKER**. CARECA RIFLES THE SOUTH AMERICANS AHEAD BUT PLATINI IS ON HAND TO **LEVEL** THE SCORES.

DESPITE THE **SWELTERING** HEAT, THE SECOND-HALF PACE IS UNRELENTING. IN THE 71ST MINUTE, **VETERAN** ZICO, ON THE FIELD FOR ONLY SIXTY SECONDS, **MISSES** A PENALTY FOR BRAZIL.

THE TIE IS FORCED INTO **EXTRA-TIME**. FOUR MINUTES FROM THE END, BRAZILIAN 'KEEPER CARLOS **CYNICALLY** CHECKS BELLONE - BUT THE FRENCHMAN IS UNABLE TO PROFIT FROM THE **ADVANTAGE** PLAYED BY THE REFEREE.

SHOOT-OUT LOSERS IN '82, FRANCE **EMERGE** VICTORIOUS THIS TIME ROUND. FOR THE BRAZILIANS, ITS TEARS AND **THOUGHTS** OF WHAT **MIGHT** HAVE BEEN.

'Happiness is not having lost your last game' - Michel Platini

TWO OTHER QUARTER-FINALS ARE **CONCLUDED** BY SHOOT-OUTS. BELGIUM OUST SPAIN AND THE **UNCONVINCING** WEST GERMANS SHADE OUT HOSTS MEXICO.

THE LAST QUARTER-FINAL IS A POTENTIALLY-**EXPLOSIVE** MEETING OF ENGLAND AND ARGENTINA. AFTER 57 GOAL-LESS MINUTES, ENGLAND'S HODGE **SLICES** A CLEARANCE **HIGH** INTO HIS OWN BOX.

GOALKEEPER SHILTON **CHARGES** OUT TO PUNCH CLEAR BUT MARADONA'S **FIST** BEATS HIM TO THE BALL. ENGLAND PROTEST BUT THE TUNISIAN REF **LETS** THE GOAL STAND.

FIVE MINUTES **LATER,** THE LITTLE ARGENTINE SCORES A GOAL AS **MEMORABLE** AS HIS FIRST WAS CONTROVERSIAL. HE LEAVES THREE ENGLAND DEFENDERS **TRAILING** BEFORE NETTING FROM EIGHT YARDS.

THE ENGLISH **REPLY** IS TOO LITTLE, TOO LATE, ALTHOUGH LINEKER'S **NEAT** HEADER MAKES HIM THE TOURNAMENT'S TOP **SCORER.**

IN THE **SEMI-FINALS,** THE WEST GERMANS ONCE AGAIN HAVE THE **MEASURE** OF FRANCE WHOSE MUCH-VAUNTED MIDFIELD IS **STIFLED** BY TIGHT-MARKING. ROLFF STICKS TO PLATINI LIKE **GLUE.**

A **TERRIBLE** ERROR FROM FRENCH 'KEEPER BATS ALLOWS BREHME TO **OPEN** THE SCORING. VOLLER'S LATE SECOND GOAL IS **ACADEMIC.** WEST GERMANY ARE IN THE FINAL FOR A RECORD **FIFTH** TIME.

IN MEXICO CITY, BELGIUM **KNOW** THEIR ONLY HOPE AGAINST ARGENTINA IS TO **CROWD OUT** MARADONA. BUT HE'S PROVING UNCONTAINABLE. IN 51 MINUTES, HE DARTS **THROUGH** TO JAB HIS SIDE INTO THE LEAD.

'The first goal against England was scored a little bit by the head of Maradona and a little bit by the hand of God!' - Diego Maradona

TWELVE MINUTES LATER, MARADONA TURNS ON THE INDIVIDUAL **BRILLIANCE** THAT'S HIS STOCK-IN-TRADE. HE SPURTS PAST THREE DEFENDERS BEFORE **CLIPPING** A SHOT **ACROSS** PFAFF - 2-0 TO ARGENTINA.

NOW **ONLY** THE GERMANS CAN HALT MARADONA. MATTHAUS IS DETAILED TO **MAN-MARK** HIM IN THE FINAL.

IN **22 MINUTES**, THE ARGENTINIAN SKIPPER FINDS ENOUGH SPACE TO HELP WIN A FREE-KICK. SCHUMACHER **MISJUDGES** THE FLIGHT OF BURRUCHAGA'S CENTRE AND BROWN HEADS INTO THE **GAPING** NET - 1-0.

JUST AFTER HALF-TIME, THINGS TURN **EVEN BLEAKER** FOR WEST GERMANY. ENRIQUE FEEDS VALDANO AND THE **TALL** STRIKER COOLLY **STEERS** IN A SECOND GOAL.

BUT **BRINKMANSHIP** IS THE GERMANS' SPECIALITY. SEVENTEEN MINUTES FROM TIME, VOLLER **TOUCHES ON** A CORNER AND RUMMENIGGE SLIDES IN TO MAKE IT 2-1.

THE EUROPEANS ARE **GALVANISED** BY THAT GOAL. EIGHT MINUTES LATER, AN ALMOST-**IDENTICAL** CORNER PLAY ENDS WITH VOLLER HEADING THE **EQUALISER**.

EXTRA-TIME? MARADONA HAS **OTHER** IDEAS. HE SUDDENLY SENDS BURRUCHAGA **CLEAR** WITH AN INCISIVE THROUGH BALL. SCHUMACHER **DASHES** OUT BUT THE MIDFIELDER'S TOUCH IS **PERFECTION** - 3-2.

FEW CAN **BEGRUDGE** ARGENTINA THEIR VICTORY. THE TOURNAMENT'S **MOST CONSISTENT** TEAM, THEY'VE BEEN SUPERBLY LED BY A MAN OF 5FT 6INS WHO'S **STOOD** HEAD-AND-SHOULDERS ABOVE EVERYONE - DIEGO ARMANDO **MARADONA**.

'Little man, you've had a busy day' - Song title, 1934

Group A

	P	W	D	L	F	A	Pts
Argentina	3	2	1	0	6	2	5
Italy	3	1	2	0	5	4	4
Bulgaria	3	0	2	1	2	4	2
South Korea	3	0	1	2	4	7	1

Group B

	P	W	D	L	F	A	Pts
Mexico	3	2	1	0	4	2	5
Paraguay	3	1	2	0	4	3	4
Belgium	3	1	1	1	5	5	3
Iraq	3	0	0	3	1	4	0

Group C

	P	W	D	L	F	A	Pts
USSR	3	2	1	0	9	1	5
France	3	2	1	0	5	1	5
Hungary	3	1	0	2	2	9	2
Canada	3	0	0	3	0	5	0

Group D

	P	W	D	L	F	A	Pts
Brazil	3	3	0	0	5	0	6
Spain	3	2	0	1	5	2	4
Northern Ireland	3	0	1	2	2	6	1
Algeria	3	0	1	2	1	5	1

Group E

	P	W	D	L	F	A	Pts
Denmark	3	3	0	0	9	1	6
West Germany	3	1	1	1	3	4	3
Uruguay	3	0	2	1	2	7	2
Scotland	3	0	1	2	1	3	1

Group F

	P	W	D	L	F	A	Pts
Morocco	3	1	2	0	3	1	4
England	3	1	1	1	3	1	3
Poland	3	1	1	1	1	3	3
Portugal	3	1	0	2	2	4	2

Second Round

Mexico	2	Bulgaria	0
USSR	3	Belgium	4
(aet)			
Brazil	4	Poland	0
Argentina	1	Uruguay	0
Italy	0	France	2
Morocco	0	West Germany	1
England	3	Paraguay	0
Spain	5	Denmark	1

Quarter-finals

Brazil	1	France	1
(aet – France won on penalties)			
West Germany	0	Mexico	0
(aet – West Germany won on penalties)			
Argentina	2	England	1
Belgium	1	Spain	1
(aet – Belgium won on penalties)			

Semi-finals

West Germany	2	France	0
Argentina	2	Belgium	0

Third place play-off

France	4	Belgium	2
(aet)			

Final

Argentina	3	West Germany	2

A qualified doctor, **Carlos Bilardo** had a very different footballing pedigree from his predecessor as national coach – Cesar Menotti.

The most successful part of Bilardo's playing career was spent as an abrasive midfielder with the infamous Estudiantes de La Plata – a club which created new dimensions in gamesmanship during the late 1960s.

After hanging up his boots, Bilardo coached in Colombia and also led Estudiantes to the 1982 Argentinian League title.

He succeeded Menotti in 1983 but Argentina's unimpressive results generated pressure to remove him prior to the 1986 World Cup.

Nicknamed 'Big nose' by less-than-subtle fans, Bilardo stayed on mainly because of support from FA president Julio Grondona.

In the end, he had the last laugh as his Maradona-inspired team raced to a famous victory in Mexico.

Bilardo had intelligently moulded a compact side which provided the perfect support system for the extra-special talents of his star player.

When the team returned from Mexico, banners all over Buenos Aires proclaimed: 'Sorry, Big nose – and thanks!'

Although Argentina continued to disappoint outside of the World Cup, Bilardo performed a near-miracle by taking an injury-hit, veteran squad to the 1990 Final in Rome.

He retired after that tournament in order to spend more time with his family but many doubted his ability to stay away from his number-one passion of football.

They were proved right when, two years after 'quitting', Bilardo returned as manager of Spanish club Sevilla where he teamed up once again with World Cup hero Maradona.

● West Germany played in an **alternative** strip of green in the 1986 World Cup Final – the only time they have had to change from their usual white-and-black colours in their six appearances in the Final. England (red in 1966) and Brazil (blue in 1958) are so far the only nations to have won the World Cup in a change strip.

● The kits worn by competing teams in the 1994 finals will include two **new features** to aid identification. Jerseys will be numbered on the front as well as the back and the player's name will also be marked (in 7.5 cm high letters) above the rear number.

● The first **widespread** use of numbers came in the 1954 World Cup but their use has not always facilitated identification. For example in 1978, Argentina played their first round matches wearing thin three-lined numbers which were almost **indecipherable** against their light blue and white jerseys. Much to the relief of TV commentators, the Argentinians adopted more solid all-black numbering for their later games.

● In 1970, FIFA ruled that any player designated the **No.13 shirt** could wear a blank jersey if he was superstitious. Ironically, Gerd Muller banged in ten goals sporting the 'unlucky' number.

● The Laws of the Game state quite clearly that players must wear appropriate **footwear** but Brazil's Leonidas seemed oblivious to this during the epic match with Poland of 1938. Perturbed by the stickiness of the increasingly-sodden pitch, the star striker suddenly decided that he would be better off without his boots. However, Swedish referee Eklind was having none of it and promptly ordered him to get them back on.

● In 1950, India **refused** to participate in the World Cup after FIFA announced that all players would have to wear boots in the finals.

● Most-inappropriate World Cup **kit choice** of all-time must belong to the Scotland team which played Uruguay in 1954. Despite the 100-degree heat in Basle, the Scots wore thick, woolly jerseys with long sleeves. According to wing-half Tommy Docherty: 'You'd have thought we were going on an expedition to the Antarctic!'

● Others who have had **problems** with their kit include Italian captain Giuseppe Meazza and the French national team. Seconds after he had converted a vital penalty in the 1938 tournament, Meazza suffered the embarrassment of his shorts falling down round his ankles. The French meanwhile had to play their 1978 match with Hungary in borrowed green-and-white striped jerseys after both teams had turned up with only white tops.

● Cameroon's green, red and yellow outfit was rated top of the 1990 strip collection by **fashion** designer John Galliano. 'A real cool look', he called it. But the Africans' success in *Italia '90* brought a headache for table soccer manufacturers Subbuteo who were inundated with requests for team sets painted in the Cameroon colours.

ITALY

1990 ITALY

IN 1990 THE TOURNAMENT **RETURNS** TO THE **CLASSIC** FOOTBALLING COUNTRY OF ITALY. 'NO-ONE WILL SLEEP' SINGS **SOCCER-LOVING** OPERA STAR LUCIANO PAVAROTTI.

ARGENTINA MANAGER BILARDO CERTAINLY DOESN'T SLUMBER WELL AFTER THE **OPENING** MATCH. HIS SIDE ARE **STUNNED** BY A SUPERB HEADER FROM CAMEROON'S OMAM BIYICK.

THE CUP **HOLDERS** HAVE AGAIN TO CALL ON THE 'HAND OF GOD' TO **HELP** THEM PROGRESS. THIS TIME, MARADONA'S RIGHT ARM **PREVENTS** A GOAL FOR THE SOVIET UNION.

MEANWHILE, IN ROME, A **STAR** IS BORN. **CROP-HAIRED** SICILIAN 'TOTO' SCHILLACI BECOMES THE TOAST OF ITALY WITH HIS **LATE** WINNER AGAINST AUSTRIA

PLAYING SLICK **ONE-TOUCH** FOOTBALL, THE HOSTS ADVANCE TO THE SECOND ROUND IN STYLE. THE USA GAIN **CREDIT** HOWEVER, BY **RESTRICTING** THEM TO A SINGLE-GOAL VICTORY.

PARADOXICALLY, THE FIRST SURPRISE RESULT OF *ITALIA '90* IS ALMOST **PREDICTABLE**. SCOTLAND, NOTORIOUSLY IMPOTENT AGAINST **LESSER** TEAMS, COME A CROPPER IN THEIR GAME WITH **COSTA RICA**.

IN MILAN, WEST GERMANY **SERVE** NOTICE OF THEIR **INTENTIONS** WITH A 4-1 DEMOLITION JOB ON YUGOSLAVIA. MIDFIELDER MATTHAUS **LEADS** THE CHARGE WITH **TWO** POWERFULLY-STRUCK GOALS.

THE UNITED ARAB EMIRATES **PROVIDE** EVEN **LESS** RESISTANCE FOR MATTHAUS AND CO. AND ARE ALMOST **WASHED AWAY** IN THE THUNDERSTORM. BUT THERE'S CONSOLATION FOR KHALID MUBARAK - HIS GOAL WINS HIM A **ROLLS-ROYCE** BACK HOME.

'All roads lead to Rome' - Traditional

IN THE **TOP** SECOND ROUND MATCH, WEST GERMANY FACE EUROPEAN CHAMPIONS HOLLAND. AN **ILL-TEMPERED** FIRST-HALF TANGLE BETWEEN VOLLER AND RIJKAARD SEES **BOTH** MEN ORDERED OFF.

DEPRIVED OF HIS STRIKING PARTNER, GERMANY'S **KLINSMANN** PLAYS THE GAME OF HIS LIFE. IN THE 50TH MINUTE, HIS **DELICATE** FINISH SETS UP A CRUCIAL VICTORY FOR BECKENBAUER'S SIDE.

IN A **CLASH** OF THE SOUTH AMERICAN HEAVYWEIGHTS, BRAZIL DO **EVERYTHING** BUT SCORE AGAINST ARGENTINA. IN THE END, THEY ARE **BEATEN** BY SOME MARADONA MAGIC - THE LITTLE MAN RELEASES CANIGGIA WHO LANDS THE **KILLER** BLOW.

ELSEWHERE, **38-YEAR-OLD** ROGER MILLA CONFIRMS HIS PLACE IN WORLD CUP **FOLKLORE**. THE CAMEROON'S SUPER SUB ROBS COLOMBIA'S **SWEEPER-KEEPER** HIGUITA TO NET THE SECOND OF TWO **SENSATIONAL** MATCH-WINNING GOALS.

JOINING THE AFRICANS AS FIRST-TIME QUARTER-FINALISTS ARE THE **REPUBLIC** OF IRELAND. BONNER'S SHOOT-OUT SAVE IS THE **KEY MOMENT** AGAINST ROMANIA.

THE IRISH **ADVENTURE** ENDS IN THE STIFLING HEAT OF ROME'S OLYMPIC STADIUM. A **PREDATORY** STRIKE FROM ITALY'S SCHILLACI IS ALL THAT **SEPARATES** THE SIDES IN AN ABSORBING MATCH.

THE **PICK** OF THE QUARTER-FINALS IS UNQUESTIONABLY THE CAMEROON-ENGLAND **TIE**. AFTER GOING BEHIND, THE AFRICAN LIONS **STORM** INTO THE LEAD IN THE 65TH MINUTE.

ENGLAND ARE **ROCKING** ON THEIR HEELS AND NEED GARY LINEKER, THEIR GOALSCORER-SUPREME, TO **RESCUE** THEM WITH **TWO** PENALTY GOALS.

'At least the world knows who we are now' - Roger Milla

IT'S A **HEAVY-DUTY** SEMI-FINAL LINE-UP. MARADONA, A HERO AT HIS **ITALIAN** CLUB NAPOLI, **CONTROVERSIALLY** APPEALS TO THE FANS THERE TO BACK ARGENTINA **AGAINST** THEIR OWN COUNTRY.

INEXCUSABLY THOUGH, THE *AZZURRI* SIT BACK **TENTATIVELY**. IN 68 MINUTES, THIS COSTS THEM DEAR WHEN **BLOND** BOMBSHELL CANIGGIA FLICKS HOME AN **EQUALISER**.

BUT THE NEAPOLITANS **REFUSE** HIS **IMPERTINENT** REQUEST AND REJOICE WITH THE REST OF ITALY WHEN **SCHILLACI** PUTS THE HOSTS IN FRONT.

NEITHER SIDE CAN **MUSTER** ANOTHER GOAL AND THE MATCH IS DECIDED BY THE NOW-ALL-TOO-**PREVALENT** PENALTY SHOOT-OUT. TENSION GETS THE BETTER OF ITALY'S **DONADONI** AND SERENA.

GOYCOCHEA, **ORIGINALLY** A SECOND-CHOICE GOALKEEPER, IS ARGENTINA'S **HERO.** 50 MILLION ITALIAN **HEARTS** ARE BROKEN.

BUT TEN MINUTES FROM **TIME**, THE ENGLISH **DESERVEDLY** DRAW LEVEL. LINEKER CLINICALLY PUNISHES **CONFUSION** IN THE GERMAN DEFENCE.

TURIN **WITNESSES** ANOTHER DRAMATIC SEMI-FINAL. WEST GERMANY DRAW FIRST BLOOD WHEN BREHME'S **DEFLECTED** FREE-KICK LOOPS OVER ENGLAND 'KEEPER SHILTON.

THE ENSUING EXTRA-TIME PRODUCES A **POIGNANT** MOMENT. YOUNG ENGLAND STAR PAUL GASCOIGNE **BURSTS** INTO TEARS WHEN A YELLOW CARD MEANS HE'LL **MISS** THE NEXT MATCH.

'See Naples and die!' - Traditional

GAZZA'S TEARS ARE NOT THE **ONLY** ONES SHED ON THE NIGHT. ENGLAND'S PEARCE AND WADDLE ARE **INCONSOLABLE** AFTER THEIR SHOOT-OUT BLUNDERS LET THE **GERMANS** GO THROUGH.

IN THE FIRST-EVER '**REPEAT**' FINAL, WEST GERMANY ARE HOT FAVOURITES TO **EXACT** REVENGE FOR THEIR 1986 DEFEAT. 40,000 OF THEIR **COUNTRYMEN** ARE AMONG THE CROWD IN ROME.

ARGENTINA'S **CHANCES** HAVE BEEN MADE ALL THE SLIMMER BY THE **SUSPENSION** OF STRIKER CANIGGIA. WHERE WILL AN ARGENTINIAN GOAL **COME** FROM NOW?

IN A **POOR** SPECTACLE, ARGENTINA APPEAR CONTENT TO **DEFEND** AND TAKE THEIR CHANCES IN A SHOOT-OUT. THEIR **SPOILING** TACTICS ARE **UNSUBTLE** AND, IN THE 68TH MINUTE, MONZON BECOMES THE FIRST MAN TO BE **RED-CARDED** IN A FINAL.

THE GERMANS ARE CLEARLY THE **BETTER** TEAM BUT THEIR **MODE** OF VICTORY IS DUBIOUS. IN THE 85TH MINUTE, VOLLER **TUMBLES** IN THE BOX AND THE WEAK MEXICAN REFEREE **AWARDS** A PENALTY.

FULL-BACK ANDY BREHME IS **ENTRUSTED** WITH THE RESPONSIBILITY. AS HUNDREDS OF **FLASH-LIGHTS** SPARKLE, HE CARRIES OUT HIS TASK WITH **APLOMB**.

TWO MINUTES LATER, DEZOTTI **FOLLOWS** MONZON INTO AN **EARLY** BATH AND ARGENTINA'S DISCIPLINE **EVAPORATES**. THE REFEREE IS **JOSTLED** AND A WHINGING MARADONA IS BOOKED.

THE FINAL WHISTLE IS A **RELIEF** TO EVERYONE. LOTHAR MATTHAUS, THE **DIGNIFIED** WEST GERMAN CAPTAIN, COLLECTS THE FIFA WORLD CUP - A JUST **REWARD** FOR THE **QUALITY** OF HIS TEAM'S PERFORMANCES IN THE EARLIER ROUNDS OF THE TOURNAMENT.

'It's a pity that Argentina didn't want to participate' - German team chief Franz Beckenbauer

Group A

	P	W	D	L	F	A	Pts
Italy	3	3	0	0	4	0	6
Czechoslovakia	3	2	0	1	6	3	4
Austria	3	1	0	2	2	3	2
USA	3	0	0	3	2	8	0

Group B

	P	W	D	L	F	A	Pts
Cameroon	3	2	0	1	3	5	4
Romania	3	1	1	1	4	3	3
Argentina	3	1	1	1	3	2	3
USSR	3	1	0	2	4	4	2

Group C

	P	W	D	L	F	A	Pts
Brazil	3	3	0	0	4	1	6
Costa Rica	3	2	0	1	3	2	4
Scotland	3	1	0	2	2	3	2
Sweden	3	0	0	3	3	6	0

Group D

	P	W	D	L	F	A	Pts
West Germany	3	2	1	0	10	3	5
Yugoslavia	3	2	0	1	6	5	4
Colombia	3	1	1	1	3	2	3
UAE	3	0	0	3	2	11	0

Group E

	P	W	D	L	F	A	Pts
Spain	3	2	1	0	5	2	5
Belgium	3	2	0	1	6	3	4
Uruguay	3	1	1	1	2	3	3
South Korea	3	0	0	3	1	6	0

Group F

	P	W	D	L	F	A	Pts
England	3	1	2	0	2	1	4
Rep. of Ireland	3	0	3	0	2	2	3
Holland	3	0	3	0	2	2	3
Egypt	3	0	2	1	1	2	2

Second Round

Cameroon (aet)	2	Colombia	1
Czechoslovakia	4	Costa Rica	1
Argentina	1	Brazil	0
West Germany	2	Holland	1
Rep. of Ireland	0	Romania	0
(aet – Ireland won on penalties)			
Italy	2	Uruguay	0
Spain (aet)	1	Yugoslavia	2
England (aet)	1	Belgium	0

Quarter-finals

Yugoslavia	0	Argentina	0
(aet – Argentina won on penalties)			
Italy	1	Rep. of Ireland	0
West Germany	1	Czechoslovakia	0
Cameroon (aet)	2	England	3

Semi-finals

Argentina	1	Italy	1
(aet – Argentina won on penalties)			
West Germany	1	England	1
(aet – West Germany won on penalties)			

Third place play-off

Italy	2	England	1

Final

West Germany	1	Argentina	0

Franz Beckenbauer has a firm place in the World Cup's Hall of Fame.

Reverently known as 'The Kaiser', he was one of the game's most complete footballers and won practically every available honour with West Germany and his club side Bayern Munich.

Beckenbauer began as a driving midfielder but later switched, with great effect, to the role of sweeper and it was from this position that he inspired his country to the epic win over Holland in 1974.

After winding down his illustrious playing career with New York Cosmos and SV Hamburg, 'Kaiser Franz' was tempted to utilise his vast experience in the area of management.

In 1984, he was appointed West German team chief and achieved a notable success in guiding a fairly mediocre squad to the runners-up spot in the 1986 World Cup.

While in Mexico, he did much to set a new managerial fashion by standing up alongside the trainer's bench during his team's matches.

Four years later, the Beckenbauer legend was to expand further when West Germany's victory in *Italia '90* made him the first man to have captained and then coached a World Cup winning side.

Although Beckenbauer himself admitted that his 1990 team was less spectacular than the side of '74, their team-work and movement provided an exemplary lesson in how modern soccer should be played.

As arranged, Beckenbauer then passed over control of the national side to Berti Vogts and, except for a brief spell as technical director at Marseille, has since restricted himself to the less-taxing role of football consultant.

● Italian fans were obviously bitterly disappointed at their team's exit in the 1990 semi-finals but at least their brave efforts spared them the **treatment** handed out to the *Azzurri* of 1966. When the unsuccessful squad sneaked into Genoa Airport in the middle of the night, they were 'welcomed' by outraged supporters who bombarded them with insults and rotten tomatoes.

● One of the strangest allegations made during *Italia '90* came from Brazilian full-back Branco who claimed that he was **drugged** when he drank from an Argentinian water-bottle during the teams' second round clash in Turin. Not surprisingly, the Argentine officials vehemently denied the claim.

● Two World Cup heroes of **yesteryear** who did not fare so well off the field were Alex Villaplane and Joe Gaetjens. In 1944, Villaplane, captain of France's 1930 team, was shot by the Resistance as a collaborator while Gaetjens, the USA's goal-hero of 1950, 'disappeared' in his native Haiti during the repressive regime of 'Papa Doc' Duvalier.

● Sadly, the original Jules Rimet trophy itself came to a sticky end in 1983. It was **stolen** from its permanent home in Brazil and is thought to have been melted down. The Brazilian Football Association have since replaced it with a duplicate.

● One of the most amusing World Cup incidents of all time occurred during the 1974 tournament. At the start of the finals, a German company had provided each squad with a **luxury coach** to shuttle them between matches and venues. After Zaire had been eliminated, a representative of the company called to collect his bus only to discover that the squad had already left and were merrily speeding down the autobahn towards Africa!

● Amazingly, over **five tonnes** of paper were required to print the tickets for the 1966 World Cup, while 30 tonnes were needed to print the sales brochures and application forms.

● How times change! In the first World Cup in 1930, only three of the competing players were based at a club in a **different country** from the one they represented in the tournament. Sixty years later, all 22 of the Republic of Ireland's squad were playing their club soccer outside of the Emerald Isle.

● Colombia's qualification for the 1990 finals set up a welcome opportunity for the USA's **Drug Enforcement Agency**. The American sleuths used surveillance equipment at Colombia's matches to track down several previously-elusive drug barons.

● It was not without justification that the famous Liverpool manager Bill Shankly once said: 'Football's not a matter of life and death – it's **more important** than that'. In 1950, three Uruguayan fans died of heart-attacks while listening to the final pool decider against Brazil and, in 1978, a Mexican fan committed suicide following his team's poor showing in Argentina. Also that year, some decidedly dissatisfied supporters threatened to blow up the headquarters of the Mexican FA!

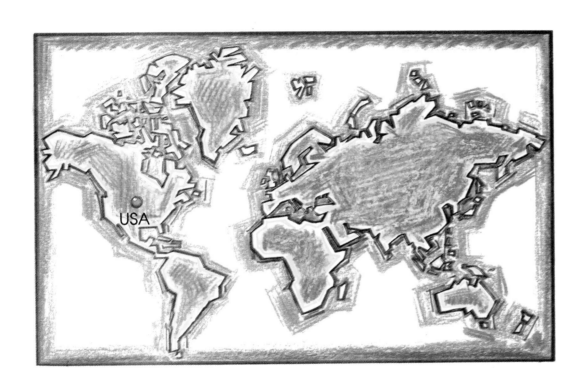

PREVIEW: USA '94

● THE FINAL FRONTIER

Sixty-four years after the first tournament in Uruguay, the world's football elite meet again, in the United States, to contest the title of World Champions. The event has come a long way from its humble origins in 1930 and USA '94 has the potential to be the greatest World Cup of all.

The Americans are ideally suited to maintain the huge off-field effort required to accommodate teams and supporters for the month-long duration of the tournament. And, although the USA has little tradition as a soccer nation, the FIFA World Cup is the perfect vehicle to catapult the game onto the major sporting agenda of the country.

The organising committee of *World Cup USA 1994* have no doubts that they can fulfil their dual mission – to stage the finest World Cup ever and leave a legacy for soccer in its last great unconquered territory.

● SOCCER IN THE STATES

Association Football has, to say the least, had a chequered history in the USA. For some reason, the Americans have never been able to establish a professional soccer league of any durability.

Since 1920, there have been the ASL, the EPL, the GASL, the ISL, the NPSL, the NASL, the CSL, the USL, the MISL (which became the MSL) and the APSL!

Probably the best known league was the NASL (North American Soccer League) in which several world superstars such as Pele (below), Franz Beckenbauer and Johan Cruyff played before large audiences in the major US cities. The NASL eventually collapsed in 1985.

Despite the problems encountered with professional competitions, soccer is very much alive at grass roots level in the US. It's estimated that approximately16 million Americans (37% of them female) currently play the game and it's second only to basketball as the most popular youth sport.

● FOR A FEW DOLLARS MORE

Commercially, World Cup '94 promises to be a major success. It looks likely that all 3.6 million tickets will be sold (2.3 million within the USA, 1.3 million internationally).

The prices range from $25, for the cheapest first round seats, to $475 for the most expensive places at the Final. Total sales could rake in over $200 million.

In addition, *World Cup USA 1994* has long since sold out its 'Official Sponsor' category and its 'Marketing Partner' programmes (to the likes of Adidas and American Airlines).

Officially-licensed World Cup merchandise – T-shirts, toys, novelty items etc. – will carry the official 1994 logo and/or the mascot, a football-playing cartoon pup named 'Striker'.

The organisers are therefore very confident of making a substantial profit – possibly around $25 million. Moreover, with well over one million foreign fans and media people visiting the country, it's estimated that the tournament could be worth as much as $4 billion to the US economy.

● THE VENUES

The naming of the stadia for the 1994 FIFA World Cup was the final step in a multi-stage venue selection procedure which took more than two years to complete.

At one time there were 32 cities, stretching from Honolulu to Boston, which were interested in hosting matches in the tournament. An extensive touring and inspection programme by the organisers finally culminated in March 1992 with the announcement of the nine chosen venues.

The Pontiac Silverdome, on the outskirts of Detroit.

In June '92, it was decided that Chicago would host the opening ceremony on June 17, 1994 while the Pasadena Rose Bowl (near Los Angeles) would stage the Final, one month later.

In the first round matches, each of the nine venues will be divided into groups of three with Los Angeles, San Francisco and Detroit to host Groups A and B; Chicago, Boston and Dallas to host Groups C and D; while New York, Orlando and Washington will host Groups E and F.

● ALL THE ACTION - LIVE

In June 1992, FIFA and the USA '94 organising committee reached an unprecedented agreement with ABC Sports and ESPN Cable on the televising of the 52-game World Cup tournament in America itself.

ABC Sports will broadcast 11 matches 'live', including two of the United States' first round games and the Championship game (that's what the Americans call the Final). ESPN will televise 41 matches, including a US first round game, both semi-finals and the third place play-off.

Interestingly, it will be the European Broadcasting Union (EBU) which will assume responsibility for the television coverage of all 52 games. The EBU was selected as 'host broadcaster' because of its experience in televising football.

It's anticipated that as many as 180 nations will take pictures from the tournament with some 31.2 billion people watching in total. The Final is expected to have a TV audience approaching two billion.

● THE QUALIFYING COMPETITION

A total of 141 nations entered the 1994 World Cup. Since Puerto Rico defeated the Dominican Republic 2-1 on March 21, 1992, more than 500 qualification matches have been played in FIFA's six world zones, called Confederations. Both the number of entrants and the number of qualifying games are new records for the tournament.

After two years of these qualifying matches, 22 teams have emerged to challenge defending champions Germany and the host nation, USA, for the 15th FIFA World Cup.

Europe will be represented by 13 countries while Africa, partly on account of the superb showing of Cameroon in *Italia '90*, will for the first time be represented by three sides.

Sadly, tragedy hit the qualifying competition in April 1993, when the entire Zambian team was killed in a plane crash while travelling to an away tie in Senegal.

● **THE AMERICAN DREAM**

No matter the sport, the American public loves a winner. But for the US national soccer team, a home success in the 1994 World Cup is likely to prove a tall order.

Since their side's creditable performance in *Italia '90*, the US Soccer Federation have channelled their efforts into producing a squad capable of competing with the cream of world football.

In 1991, the appointment as coach of Yugoslav Bora Milutinovic brought a fresh new philosophy and atmosphere to the national scene.

It could be argued that Milutinovic has enjoyed a luxury not afforded to most international managers. He has been able to operate in relative peace – largely because the American media have not thus far shown much interest in their team.

But the enormity of his task should not be underestimated. He has, after all, had to put together a side in a country which has no serious professional league and whose top players are all based with European clubs.

Several of them have enjoyed success at national level – Thomas Dooley won a German Championship medal with Kaiserslautern in 1991 while, in May 1993, John Harkes became the first American to play in the English FA Cup Final.

Fielding only home-based players, the US team's early 1993 results were disappointing, but it was a very different story when the exiles returned for the four-nation US Cup in June.

After going down 2-0 to Brazil, the Americans sent shock waves around the soccer world with a 2-0 victory over England in Boston. They followed that by slamming three goals past world champions Germany in a narrow defeat.

Form like that should at least ensure that the US side progresses beyond the first stage of World Cup '94 and after that, who knows?

What is certain is that there are no clear favourites to win the tournament. For the first time in World Cup history, neither the Europeans nor the Latin Americans have the advantage of playing in their own continent.

On June 17, speculation will give way to action. The world's top footballers will then write an exciting new chapter in this great sporting story.